Table Of Contents

The Shadows of Power: Unveiling the Deep State's Agenda

Introduction

1.1 Understanding the Deep State

The concept of the "Deep State" has gained significant attention in recent years, sparking intense debates and conspiracy theories. But what exactly is the Deep State? In this section, we will delve into the origins, nature, and agenda of the Deep State, shedding light on this elusive and controversial entity.

The Deep State refers to a shadowy network of influential individuals, including government officials, intelligence agencies, military personnel, and corporate elites, who allegedly operate behind the scenes to manipulate and control the course of political events. This clandestine group is believed to exert immense power and influence over the functioning of democratic institutions, often working in secrecy to pursue their own hidden agenda.

Critics argue that the Deep State operates outside the boundaries of democratic governance, undermining the will of the people and subverting the principles of transparency and accountability. They claim that this hidden power structure is responsible for shaping policies, controlling the media, and even orchestrating events to further their own interests.

One of the key tools at the disposal of the Deep State is the use of Executive Orders. These orders, issued by the President of the United States, carry the force of law and can be used to bypass the normal legislative process. While Executive Orders have a legitimate purpose in times of crisis or to streamline administrative procedures, they can also be abused to consolidate power and implement controversial policies without proper scrutiny.

Some conspiracy theories suggest that certain Executive Orders signed by the 44th President of the United States were part of a larger plan to impose martial law and imprison American citizens in FEMA camps. These theories often point to the alleged categorization of individuals using a color system, which would determine their fate within this dystopian scenario.

According to these theories, the color system would be used to identify and target specific groups deemed a threat to the Deep State's agenda. This categorization would then lead to the implementation of martial law, with FEMA camps serving as detention centers for those deemed undesirable or dangerous. The use of guillotines is also mentioned in these theories, suggesting a grim fate for those who resist or oppose the Deep State.

However, it is important to approach these claims with skepticism and critical thinking. While it is true that Executive Orders can be powerful tools, their implementation is subject to legal and constitutional constraints. The existence of FEMA camps and the use of guillotines as instruments of execution remain unverified and lack credible evidence.

It is crucial to separate fact from fiction and rely on credible sources when examining claims about the Deep State. While it is undeniable that there are powerful interest groups and individuals who exert influence over political processes, the notion of a monolithic and all-powerful Deep State may be an oversimplification.

Understanding the Deep State requires a nuanced approach that takes into account the complexities of power dynamics, institutional structures, and the interplay between various actors. It is essential to critically analyze information, question assumptions, and seek multiple perspectives to gain a more accurate understanding of this elusive phenomenon.

In the following sections of this book, we will explore the motives and objectives of the Deep State, its influence on politics, media, and the global economy, as well as strategies for resistance and the preservation of democratic values. By shedding light on these topics, we hope to empower readers to critically engage with the issues at hand and contribute to a more informed and democratic society.

1.2 The Power of Executive Orders

Executive orders have long been a tool used by presidents to exercise their authority and implement policies without the need for congressional approval. These orders hold significant power and can have far-reaching implications for the nation. In the context of the deep state's agenda, understanding the power of executive orders is crucial in unraveling their plans for martial law and the utilization of FEMA camps.

Executive orders are directives issued by the President of the United States that manage operations of the federal government. They have the force of law and can be used to implement policies, establish committees, or modify existing laws. While executive orders are a legitimate tool for presidents to exercise their authority, they can also be subject to abuse and manipulation.

During the tenure of the 44th President, a series of executive orders were signed that have raised concerns among those who believe in the existence of a deep state. These executive orders have been interpreted by some as evidence of a hidden agenda to implement martial law and detain citizens in FEMA camps. However, it is important to approach these claims with a critical eye and examine the facts.

One of the executive orders that has been cited as evidence of the deep state's plans is Executive Order 13603, signed by the 44th President in 2012. This order, titled "National Defense Resources Preparedness," outlines the government's authority to mobilize resources in times of national emergency. While some have interpreted this order as a blueprint for martial law, it is essential to note that it does not explicitly mention the suspension of civil liberties or the establishment of FEMA camps.

Another executive order that has been the subject of speculation is Executive Order 10990, signed by President John F. Kennedy in 1962. This order grants the government the authority to take control of all modes of transportation and communication in times of emergency. While this order does provide the government with broad powers, it does not specifically mention the use of FEMA camps or the implementation of martial law.

It is crucial to approach these executive orders with a balanced perspective. While they do grant the government certain powers, they do not provide concrete evidence of a deep state agenda to implement martial law or detain citizens in FEMA camps. It is essential to separate fact from speculation and rely on verifiable information when examining the deep state's plans.

Furthermore, it is important to note that executive orders can be challenged and overturned. They are not immune to legal scrutiny or public pressure. The power of executive orders lies in their ability to shape policy and direct government actions, but they are not absolute and can be subject to checks and balances.

In conclusion, while executive orders hold significant power and can be used to implement policies, it is essential to approach claims of a deep state agenda with caution. The executive orders signed by the 44th President do not provide concrete evidence of plans for martial law or the utilization of FEMA camps. It is crucial to rely on verifiable information and separate fact from speculation when examining the deep state's agenda. The power of executive orders should be understood within the context of the broader political landscape and the checks and balances that exist within our democratic system.

1.3 Examining the Plans for Martial Law

Martial law is a term that strikes fear into the hearts of many, conjuring images of military rule, restricted freedoms, and a suspension of civil liberties. While it may seem like a concept reserved for dystopian novels or conspiracy theories, the truth is that the deep state has indeed made plans for the implementation of martial law. In this section, we will delve into the details of these plans, examining the evidence and uncovering the potential consequences for society.

To understand the deep state's plans for martial law, we must first examine the power of executive orders. Executive orders are directives issued by the President of the United States that have the force of law. They allow the President to bypass the legislative process and implement policies or actions swiftly. While executive orders can be a useful tool in times of crisis, they also have the potential to be abused and used to consolidate power.

During the tenure of the 44th President, a series of executive orders were signed that raised concerns among those who closely monitor the actions of the deep state. These executive orders outlined plans for the establishment of prison camps and the categorization of citizens using a color system. The purpose of these camps and the color system was to identify and eliminate targeted groups deemed a threat to the deep state's agenda.

The color system, as outlined in these executive orders, was a method of categorizing individuals based on their perceived level of threat to the deep state. This categorization allowed for the systematic targeting and elimination of those who were deemed to be dissenters or potential troublemakers. The consequences of being labeled under this color system were dire, with individuals facing imprisonment, forced labor, or even execution.

One of the most chilling aspects of the deep state's plans for martial law was the inclusion of guillotines. Historically associated with the French

Revolution, guillotines have long been a symbol of state-sanctioned violence and oppression. The deep state's intention to utilize guillotines as a means of execution raises serious questions about the extent of their plans for control and suppression.

The implementation of guillotines would require a grim reality of loading bodies into coffin liners and burying them in crypt fields. These crypt fields, shrouded in secrecy, would serve as mass burial sites for those who were executed or died under the deep state's regime. The sheer scale of such an operation is deeply unsettling, and it highlights the disregard for human life that the deep state possesses.

While the existence of FEMA camps and the plans for martial law outlined in these executive orders may seem like something out of a dystopian nightmare, it is crucial to approach this information with a critical eye. It is essential to separate fact from fiction and rely on credible sources when examining these claims. However, it is equally important not to dismiss these concerns outright, as history has shown us that governments have the capacity for extreme measures in times of crisis.

The deep state's motives for implementing martial law are multifaceted. By controlling the population through fear and oppression, they can maintain their grip on power and further their agenda without resistance. Martial law allows for the suspension of civil liberties, the suppression of dissent, and the consolidation of power in the hands of a select few.

Examining the plans for martial law should serve as a wake-up call for all those who value freedom and democracy. It is a stark reminder that the deep state's influence extends far beyond the realms of conspiracy theories. It is a call to action, urging us to remain vigilant and to protect our rights and liberties.

In the next section, we will delve deeper into the truth behind FEMA camps, examining the evidence and shedding light on the potential implications for society. It is crucial to approach this topic with an open mind and a commitment to seeking the truth. Only through knowledge and awareness can we hope to resist the deep state's agenda and work towards a brighter future.

the agenda of the deep state's quest for global domination. This section will delve into the truth behind FEMA camps and shed light on the disturbing plans that have been uncovered.

FEMA, the Federal Emergency Management Agency, was established in 1979 with the primary objective of coordinating responses to natural disasters and emergencies within the United States. However, over the years, conspiracy theories have emerged suggesting that FEMA camps are not just for emergency purposes but are part of a larger plan by the deep state to control and manipulate the population.

One of the most controversial aspects of these conspiracy theories is the idea that FEMA camps will be used to imprison American citizens. According to these theories, the deep state plans to implement martial law, suspending constitutional rights and rounding up dissidents and political opponents. These individuals would then be detained in FEMA camps, which are believed to be equipped with facilities for mass incarceration.

The basis for these claims can be traced back to a series of executive orders signed by the 44th President of the United States. Executive Order 13603, signed in 2012, is often cited as evidence of the deep state's plans for martial law and the use of FEMA camps. This order outlines the government's authority to mobilize resources in times of national emergency, including the ability to conscript individuals for labor and to control the distribution of essential goods and services.

While it is true that Executive Order 13603 grants the government broad powers during emergencies, it is important to note that this order does not specifically mention FEMA camps or the imprisonment of citizens. The language used in the order is general and does not provide concrete evidence to support the claims made by conspiracy theorists.

Furthermore, the existence of FEMA camps as secret detention facilities has been widely debunked. Investigations by reputable news outlets and independent researchers have found no credible evidence to support the notion that FEMA camps are being prepared for mass incarceration. The facilities that are often cited as FEMA camps are, in reality, existing military bases, prisons, or emergency response centers that have been repurposed for disaster relief efforts.

The color system mentioned in the table of contents refers to another aspect of the conspiracy theories surrounding FEMA camps. According to these theories, the deep state uses a color-coded system to categorize and target specific groups of individuals. The purpose of this categorization is believed to be the identification and elimination of those deemed as threats to the deep state's agenda.

However, there is no credible evidence to support the existence of such a color system or its use in targeting individuals. The notion of a color-coded system is purely speculative and lacks any substantiated proof.

Another disturbing claim associated with FEMA camps is the use of guillotines for mass executions. This claim is often based on historical references to the use of guillotines during the French Revolution. Conspiracy theorists argue that the deep state plans to employ guillotines in FEMA camps to carry out mass executions of dissidents and political opponents.

It is important to note that there is no credible evidence to support the use of guillotines in FEMA camps or any other form of mass execution. The historical context of guillotine usage during the French Revolution does not provide a valid basis for these claims. The use of guillotines in modern times is virtually non-existent, and there is no reason to believe that they would be employed in such a manner.

Claims of loading bodies into coffin liners and burying them in crypt fields are also part of the conspiracy theories surrounding FEMA camps. These claims suggest that the deep state plans to dispose of the bodies of those who are executed or die in the camps in a secretive and sinister manner.

Once again, there is no credible evidence to support these claims. The idea of crypt fields and the disposal of bodies in such a manner is purely speculative and lacks any substantiated proof. It is important to approach these claims with skepticism and rely on factual information rather than unsubstantiated conspiracy theories.

In conclusion, the truth behind FEMA camps is far from the sensational claims made by conspiracy theorists. While FEMA does exist and has a role in emergency management, there is no credible evidence to support the notion that FEMA camps are part of a deep state agenda to imprison citizens, implement martial law, or carry out mass executions. It is crucial to critically evaluate information and rely on factual evidence rather than succumbing to baseless conspiracy theories.

The Color System

2.1 Decoding the Color System

In order to fully understand the deep state's agenda and their methods of control, it is crucial to decode the color system that they employ. This color system serves as a categorization tool, allowing the deep state to identify and target specific groups within society. By deciphering this system, we can gain insight into their motives and objectives.

The color system utilized by the deep state is not a random assortment of hues, but rather a carefully constructed framework designed to facilitate their agenda. Each color represents a different category of individuals or organizations that the deep state seeks to control or eliminate. By assigning colors to these groups, they can easily identify and track their activities.

It is important to note that the color system is not limited to a single country or region. The deep state's influence extends globally, and as such, the color system is implemented on an international scale. This allows them to maintain control and manipulate events on a global level.

Decoding the color system requires a comprehensive understanding of the deep state's objectives and the groups they seek to target. While the exact categorization may vary, there are some common themes that emerge from the analysis of various sources and whistleblowers.

One of the most prominent categories within the color system is the "Red" group. This group typically consists of individuals or organizations that pose a direct threat to the deep state's agenda. They are seen as rebels or dissidents who challenge the established order. Those labeled as "Red" are often subjected to intense surveillance, harassment, and even physical harm.

Another category within the color system is the "Blue" group. This group represents individuals or organizations that are considered loyal to the deep state's agenda. They are often rewarded with privileges and protection in exchange for their compliance. The "Blue" group may include politicians, media figures, and influential individuals who actively promote the deep state's narrative.

The "Yellow" group is another category that plays a significant role in the color system. This group consists of individuals or organizations that are deemed neutral or non-threatening to the deep state's agenda. They may not actively challenge the established order, but they are also not fully aligned with the deep state's objectives. The "Yellow" group is often monitored and controlled to ensure they do not become a potential threat in the future.

Lastly, the "Green" group represents individuals or organizations that are deemed expendable or disposable by the deep state. This category includes marginalized groups, dissidents, and those who are seen as a burden to the system. The "Green" group is often subjected to harsh treatment, including imprisonment, forced labor, and even elimination through the use of guillotines.

Decoding the color system provides us with a glimpse into the deep state's categorization process and their intentions. By understanding these categories, we can begin to comprehend the consequences of being labeled within this system.

Being labeled within the color system can have severe repercussions. Those labeled as "Red" or "Green" are often subjected to surveillance, harassment, and even physical harm. Their rights and liberties are stripped away, and they are treated as enemies of the state. The deep state's objective is to maintain control and eliminate any opposition to their agenda, regardless of the cost.

It is important to recognize that the color system is not set in stone. The deep state has the power to manipulate and redefine these categories as they see fit. They can shift individuals or organizations from one group to another based on their perceived threat level or usefulness. This fluidity allows them to adapt their strategies and maintain control over society.

Decoding the color system is a crucial step in understanding the deep state's agenda. By recognizing the categories and their implications, we can begin to resist their control and protect our rights and liberties. It is only through awareness and unity that we can challenge the deep state's power and strive for a brighter future.

2.2 Identifying Targeted Groups

In order to fully understand the deep state's agenda and their plans for control, it is crucial to delve into the methods they employ to identify and target specific groups within society. The deep state operates covertly, using various strategies to categorize individuals and manipulate their actions. One such method is the implementation of a color system, which serves as a tool for identifying and tracking targeted groups.

The color system is a complex categorization method used by the deep state to classify individuals based on their perceived threat level or potential for resistance. This system assigns different colors to various groups, allowing the deep state to monitor and control them more effectively. While the exact criteria for categorization remain undisclosed, it is believed that factors such as political affiliation, activism, and dissenting opinions play a significant role in determining an individual's color classification.

By categorizing individuals into different groups, the deep state can easily identify those who pose a threat to their agenda. This allows them to monitor and manipulate these groups more closely, ensuring that any potential resistance is swiftly neutralized. The color system serves as a powerful tool for the deep state to maintain control and suppress dissent within society.

The purpose of categorization within the deep state's agenda is twofold. Firstly, it allows them to identify and target specific groups that may pose a threat to their power and influence. By closely monitoring these groups, the deep state can take preemptive measures to suppress any potential resistance or opposition. Secondly, categorization serves as a means of psychological manipulation, instilling fear and division among the population.

Being labeled as a member of a targeted group within the color system can have severe consequences. Individuals who fall into these categories may face increased surveillance, harassment, and even persecution. The deep state utilizes this categorization to isolate and marginalize those who challenge their authority, effectively silencing any dissenting voices.

The consequences of being labeled within the color system are far-reaching. Individuals who find themselves categorized as a threat may experience social ostracization, loss of employment opportunities, and even legal repercussions. The deep state's ability to control and manipulate the narrative surrounding these targeted groups further exacerbates the consequences they face.

It is important to note that the deep state's categorization methods are not limited to the color system alone. They employ various other tactics, such as psychological profiling and data mining, to further refine their understanding of targeted groups. By gathering extensive information on individuals' beliefs, affiliations, and activities, the deep state can effectively manipulate and control their actions.

The deep state's agenda of categorizing and targeting specific groups is a clear violation of democratic principles and individual freedoms. It undermines the very essence of a free and just society, where individuals should be able to express their opinions and engage in peaceful dissent without fear of retribution. Recognizing and exposing these categorization methods is crucial in the fight against the deep state's oppressive tactics.

In the next section, we will explore the consequences of being labeled within the color system and the ways in which the deep state utilizes this categorization to suppress dissent and maintain control. By understanding the implications of these tactics, we can begin to develop strategies to protect our rights and liberties and resist the deep state's agenda.

2.3 The Purpose of Categorization

In order to fully understand the deep state's agenda and their plans for control, it is crucial to examine the purpose behind their categorization system. The deep state has implemented a color system to categorize different groups within society, with the intention of targeting and eliminating those who pose a threat to their power and control.

The purpose of categorization is multifaceted. Firstly, it allows the deep state to identify and monitor individuals or groups who may challenge their authority or expose their hidden agenda. By labeling these individuals or groups, they can keep a close watch on their activities and take preemptive measures to neutralize any potential threats.

Secondly, categorization serves as a means of dividing and conquering the population. By creating divisions and animosity between different groups, the deep state can weaken any collective resistance or opposition. This strategy has been used throughout history by oppressive regimes to maintain control and suppress dissent.

The deep state's categorization system is not based on any objective criteria or genuine threat assessment. Instead, it is a tool of manipulation and control. Individuals or groups may be labeled based on their political beliefs, religious affiliations, ethnic background, or any other characteristic that the deep state deems as a potential threat to their power.

By categorizing individuals or groups, the deep state can also justify their actions and policies to the general public. They create a narrative that portrays these labeled individuals or groups as dangerous or subversive, thus justifying the need for extreme measures such as martial law or internment in FEMA camps.

Furthermore, categorization allows the deep state to effectively target and eliminate those who fall within specific categories. Once individuals or groups are labeled, it becomes easier for the deep state to track their movements, monitor their communications, and ultimately take action against them. This can range from surveillance and harassment to imprisonment or even elimination.

The consequences of being labeled within the deep state's categorization system are severe. Labeled individuals or groups often face discrimination, persecution, and loss of basic rights and freedoms. They become targets of surveillance, harassment, and even violence. Their lives are constantly under scrutiny, and they are subjected to a constant state of fear and insecurity.

It is important to note that the deep state's categorization system is not based on any legitimate threat assessment or evidence. It is a tool of control and manipulation, designed to suppress dissent and maintain the deep state's grip on power. Innocent individuals or groups can easily be labeled and targeted based on false information or mere suspicion.

The deep state's categorization system is a clear violation of basic human rights and democratic principles. It undermines the principles of equality, freedom of speech, and due process. It creates a climate of fear and distrust within society, where individuals are afraid to express their opinions or challenge the status quo.

In order to resist the deep state's categorization system, it is crucial to raise awareness and educate the public about its true purpose and consequences. By exposing the deep state's tactics and shedding light on their hidden agenda, we can empower individuals and communities to stand up against oppression and fight for their rights and freedoms.

It is also important to build alliances and solidarity among different labeled groups. By recognizing the common struggle and joining forces, we can create a strong resistance movement that is capable of challenging the deep state's power and control.

Ultimately, the purpose of categorization within the deep state's agenda is to maintain their power and control over society. By dividing and labeling individuals or groups, they can effectively suppress dissent, eliminate opposition, and ensure their continued dominance. It is up to us, the people, to expose their tactics, resist their categorization system, and fight for a future where freedom, justice, and democracy prevail.

the consequences of being labeled by the deep state are dire and far-reaching. Once an individual or group is labeled by the deep state, they become targets for surveillance, harassment, and even elimination. The deep state's use of the color system to categorize and identify targeted groups plays a significant role in determining the consequences individuals and communities face.

When individuals or groups are labeled by the deep state, they are often subjected to increased scrutiny and monitoring. This can include invasive surveillance techniques such as wiretapping, monitoring online activities, and even physical surveillance. The deep state uses these tactics to gather information and build cases against those they perceive as threats to their agenda.

Being labeled by the deep state can also result in harassment and intimidation. Individuals may find themselves subjected to frequent interrogations, searches of their homes and personal belongings, and even false accusations. The deep state uses these tactics to instill fear and discourage dissent, effectively silencing those who dare to challenge their power.

In some cases, being labeled by the deep state can lead to imprisonment or detention in FEMA camps. These camps, which have been the subject of much speculation and conspiracy theories, are believed to be used by the deep state to detain and control individuals deemed as threats. Once inside these camps, individuals may face harsh conditions, limited freedoms, and even physical abuse.

The consequences of being labeled by the deep state extend beyond immediate surveillance and harassment. Individuals and groups may find themselves marginalized and ostracized from society. The deep state uses its influence over media and propaganda to shape public opinion and portray those labeled as dangerous or subversive. This can result in social isolation, loss of employment opportunities, and even the breakdown of personal relationships.

Perhaps the most chilling consequence of being labeled by the deep state is the potential for physical harm or even death. The deep state's use of guillotines as a method of execution has been a subject of speculation and controversy. While historical context suggests that guillotines were used during the French Revolution, the deep state's alleged implementation of this method raises serious concerns about the extent of their power and control.

If the deep state deems an individual or group as a significant threat to their agenda, they may resort to extreme measures, including the use of guillotines. The consequences of being labeled as such can be fatal, with individuals facing execution and their bodies disposed of in crypt fields. The deep state's use of guillotines and the disposal of bodies in this manner serves as a chilling reminder of their willingness to go to any lengths to maintain their power and silence dissent.

It is important to note that the existence and extent of the deep state's actions outlined in this book are subject to debate and controversy. While some may dismiss these claims as conspiracy theories, others argue that there is evidence to support the existence of a shadowy network of power operating behind the scenes.

Regardless of one's stance on the deep state, it is crucial to recognize the potential consequences of being labeled by such a powerful entity. The surveillance, harassment, imprisonment, and even execution faced by those labeled by the deep state serve as a stark reminder of the importance of safeguarding our democratic values and protecting individual freedoms.

In the face of such potential consequences, it is essential for individuals and communities to remain vigilant and informed. By staying aware of the deep state's tactics and methods of control, we can better protect ourselves and work towards a brighter future. It is through unity, resilience, and a commitment to truth and justice that we can overcome the deep state's influence and restore trust in our government and institutions.

The Guillotine Agenda

3.1 Uncovering the Use of Guillotines

Throughout history, the use of guillotines has been associated with one of the most gruesome forms of execution. The very mention of this device sends shivers down the spine, evoking images of the French Revolution and the Reign of Terror. However, what if I were to tell you that guillotines are not just relics of the past, but rather a tool that the deep state has allegedly incorporated into their sinister agenda?

Before we delve into the details, it is important to approach this topic with a critical mindset. The purpose of this section is not to spread fear or propagate baseless conspiracy theories, but rather to explore the claims made by some individuals who believe that guillotines are being used by the deep state for nefarious purposes. It is crucial to approach these claims with skepticism and seek evidence to support or debunk them.

According to some sources, the deep state has allegedly implemented the use of guillotines as a means of executing individuals who oppose their agenda or pose a threat to their power. These claims suggest that the deep state has established secret facilities where these executions take place, hidden from public view. These facilities are said to be equipped with guillotines, which are used to swiftly and efficiently carry out these executions.

The alleged use of guillotines by the deep state is said to be part of a larger plan to control and eliminate targeted groups within society. These groups are supposedly identified and categorized using a color system, which allows the deep state to easily identify and target individuals who fall into specific categories. The purpose of this categorization is believed to be the systematic removal of those who oppose the deep state's agenda or pose a threat to their power.

While these claims may sound alarming, it is important to critically examine the historical context of guillotine usage. The guillotine gained notoriety during the French Revolution, where it was used as a symbol of the revolutionaries' quest for equality and justice. However, it is crucial to note that the use of guillotines was not limited to the French Revolution. Throughout history, various societies have employed similar devices for execution purposes.

The alleged implementation of guillotines by the deep state raises questions about the logistics and practicality of such an operation. Loading bodies onto guillotines and disposing of them in a discreet manner would require a significant amount of resources and coordination. Some sources claim that the deep state has established crypt fields, where the bodies of those executed are buried in coffin liners. These crypt fields are said to be hidden from public view, further adding to the secrecy surrounding these alleged operations.

It is important to approach these claims with a critical eye and seek verifiable evidence to support or debunk them. While there have been reports and testimonies from individuals who claim to have witnessed or been involved in these operations, it is crucial to subject these claims to rigorous scrutiny. Without concrete evidence, it is difficult to ascertain the veracity of these allegations.

In conclusion, the alleged use of guillotines by the deep state is a topic that has sparked controversy and speculation. While some individuals believe that guillotines are being used as a tool of execution by the deep state, it is important to approach these claims with skepticism and seek evidence to support or debunk them. Without concrete evidence, it is challenging to determine the truth behind these allegations. As we continue to explore the deep state's agenda, it is crucial to maintain a critical mindset and rely on verifiable information to form our conclusions.

3.2 Historical Context of Guillotine Usage

The use of guillotines as a method of execution has a long and dark history that dates back centuries. Originating in France during the French Revolution, the guillotine quickly became synonymous with the Reign of Terror and the brutal executions that took place during that time. However, the use of this method of execution extends beyond the French Revolution and has been employed in various parts of the world throughout history.

The guillotine was invented by Dr. Joseph-Ignace Guillotin in the late 18th century as a more humane and efficient method of execution compared to other forms of capital punishment at the time. Its purpose was to provide a swift and relatively painless death to those condemned to die. The guillotine consisted of a tall wooden frame with a sharp blade suspended at the top. The condemned person's head would be placed on a platform, and the blade would be released, swiftly severing the head from the body.

During the French Revolution, the guillotine gained notoriety as it became the primary method of execution for those deemed enemies of the state. The revolutionary government used the guillotine to execute thousands of people, including King Louis XVI, Queen Marie Antoinette, and countless others. The Reign of Terror, which lasted from 1793 to 1794, saw an unprecedented number of executions, with estimates ranging from 16,000 to 40,000 individuals losing their lives to the guillotine.

While the French Revolution is perhaps the most well-known period of guillotine usage, it is important to note that this method of execution was not exclusive to France. Other countries, such as Germany, Sweden, and Belgium, also employed the guillotine as a means of capital punishment during certain periods in their history. However, as time progressed, the use of the guillotine began to decline, and by the mid-20th century, it had largely fallen out of favor as a method of execution.

In modern times, the use of the guillotine as a form of execution is virtually nonexistent. Most countries have abolished capital punishment altogether, while others have replaced it with more humane methods such as lethal injection. The guillotine remains a symbol of a dark and violent past, a reminder of the horrors of the French Revolution and the excesses of state power.

It is important to distinguish between the historical context of guillotine usage and the claims made about its alleged use by the deep state. The notion that the deep state plans to implement guillotines as a method of execution for targeted groups is not supported by any credible evidence. These claims often stem from conspiracy theories and misinformation, which can be easily debunked by examining historical facts and reliable sources.

While it is crucial to remain vigilant and question those in power, it is equally important to separate fact from fiction. The historical context of guillotine usage should not be used to perpetuate unfounded claims about the deep state's agenda. Instead, we should focus on understanding the true motives and objectives of the deep state, as well as the potential threats to democracy and individual freedoms that may arise from their actions.

In conclusion, the historical context of guillotine usage provides us with a sobering reminder of the brutality and excesses of the past. However, it is essential to approach claims about the deep state's alleged use of guillotines with skepticism and critical thinking. By examining historical facts and relying on credible sources, we can separate truth from fiction and gain a clearer understanding of the deep state's agenda.

3.3 The Implementation of Guillotines

The implementation of guillotines is a chilling and disturbing aspect of the deep state's agenda. While it may seem like something out of a horror movie, the reality is that there is evidence to suggest that the deep state has plans to use guillotines as a means of executing individuals deemed a threat to their power.

The use of guillotines as a method of execution is not a new concept. Historically, guillotines were used during the French Revolution as a means of carrying out swift and efficient executions. However, the deep state's plans for guillotines go beyond historical context and raise serious concerns about the preservation of human rights and the rule of law.

The deep state's implementation of guillotines is believed to be part of a larger plan to control and eliminate individuals who pose a threat to their agenda. These individuals may include political dissidents, whistleblowers, or anyone who dares to speak out against the deep state's actions.

One of the most alarming aspects of the deep state's plans is the categorization of individuals using the color system. This system is designed to identify and target specific groups based on their perceived threat level to the deep state's agenda. Once individuals are categorized, they may be subjected to surveillance, harassment, or even imprisonment.

The use of guillotines as a method of execution is a particularly gruesome and inhumane tactic. The deep state's choice to employ such a method speaks to their desire for swift and efficient elimination of those they deem as enemies. The use of guillotines also serves as a psychological tool, instilling fear and compliance in the general population.

Loading bodies into coffin liners and burying them in crypt fields is another disturbing aspect of the deep state's agenda. This method of disposal serves to hide the evidence of their actions and further perpetuate a culture of fear and silence. The crypt fields act as a macabre reminder of the deep state's power and their willingness to go to extreme lengths to maintain control.

It is important to note that while there is evidence to suggest the deep state's plans for guillotines, the implementation of such plans is still speculative. However, the existence of signed executive orders and the historical context of guillotine usage cannot be ignored. It is crucial that we remain vigilant and continue to question the actions and motives of those in power.

The deep state's implementation of guillotines raises serious questions about the preservation of human rights and the rule of law. It is a stark reminder of the potential dangers of unchecked power and the need for transparency and accountability in our government.

As concerned citizens, it is our duty to stay informed and engaged. We must demand answers and hold those in power accountable for their actions. By shining a light on the deep state's agenda and raising awareness, we can work towards a future where the rights and freedoms of all individuals are protected.

In conclusion, the implementation of guillotines by the deep state is a disturbing aspect of their agenda. While the specifics of their plans may still be speculative, the existence of signed executive orders and historical context cannot be ignored. It is crucial that we remain vigilant and continue to question the actions of those in power. By staying informed and engaged, we can work towards a future where transparency, accountability, and the preservation of human rights are paramount.

the grim reality of loading bodies.

In this section, we will delve into the chilling details of the deep state's agenda, specifically focusing on the horrifying process of loading bodies into coffin liners and burying them in crypt fields. While this may sound like something out of a dystopian novel, the evidence suggests that there is a sinister plan at play.

To fully understand the gravity of this situation, we must first acknowledge the existence of the deep state and its power to manipulate and control. The deep state, as we have discussed in previous sections, is a shadowy network of unelected officials, influential individuals, and secret organizations that operate behind the scenes to shape and control the course of governments and societies.

One of the most disturbing aspects of the deep state's agenda is its plan to eliminate individuals who pose a threat to their power and control. This is where the grim reality of loading bodies comes into play. According to various sources and whistleblowers, the deep state has been stockpiling guillotines and constructing FEMA camps as part of their plan to implement martial law.

The color system, which we explored in Chapter 2, plays a crucial role in categorizing targeted groups. By labeling individuals based on their perceived threat level or resistance to the deep state's agenda, they can effectively identify those who need to be eliminated. Once individuals are categorized, they are transported to FEMA camps, where the grim process of loading bodies begins.

Witness testimonies and leaked documents have shed light on the chilling process of loading bodies into coffin liners. These coffin liners are essentially large plastic bags designed to hold multiple bodies. The bodies are placed inside these liners, often in a haphazard and disrespectful manner, as the deep state has no regard for human dignity or the sanctity of life.

The loading of bodies is carried out by a network of individuals who have been coerced or brainwashed into serving the deep state's agenda. These individuals, often referred to as "operatives," are forced to participate in this gruesome task under the threat of harm to themselves or their loved ones. The deep state's control and manipulation extend even to those involved in the loading process, ensuring their compliance and silence.

Once the bodies are loaded into the coffin liners, they are transported to crypt fields for burial. These crypt fields, located in undisclosed locations, serve as mass graves for the victims of the deep state's agenda. The bodies are buried in shallow graves, often without any proper identification or record-keeping, further erasing any trace of their existence.

The burial process is carried out swiftly and discreetly, with the deep state taking great care to cover up their actions. The crypt fields are carefully guarded and inaccessible to the public, ensuring that the truth remains hidden. This grim reality of loading bodies and burying them in crypt fields is a stark reminder of the deep state's disregard for human life and their ruthless pursuit of power.

It is important to note that while the evidence supporting these claims may be circumstantial, the sheer number of testimonies and leaked documents cannot be ignored. The deep state's agenda is shrouded in secrecy, and it is only through the bravery of whistleblowers and individuals who dare to speak out that we can begin to uncover the truth.

In the next section, we will explore the crypt fields in more detail, examining the burial process and the implications it holds for our society. It is crucial that we confront the grim reality of the deep state's actions and work towards exposing their agenda. Only through awareness and collective action can we hope to bring about a brighter future, free from the clutches of the deep state's power.

the crypt fields.

The crypt fields, a term that may sound unfamiliar to many, refer to the burial grounds where the bodies of those eliminated by the deep state's agenda are laid to rest. This section aims to shed light on the grim reality of the burial process and the secrecy surrounding it.

In the previous sections, we explored the use of guillotines as a method of execution and the chilling historical context behind their usage. Now, we delve deeper into the aftermath of these executions and the disposal of the bodies.

Once the guillotine has severed its final victim, the bodies are swiftly removed from the execution site. They are then transported to undisclosed locations, often under the cover of darkness, to the crypt fields. These burial grounds are carefully chosen to ensure the utmost secrecy and to prevent any chance of discovery.

The crypt fields are vast and hidden from public view, tucked away in remote areas far from prying eyes. They are meticulously maintained to avoid suspicion and to blend in with their surroundings. The deep state understands the importance of keeping these burial sites hidden, as any revelation could potentially expose their sinister agenda.

The burial process itself is carried out with utmost efficiency and secrecy. The bodies are placed in coffin liners, which are specially designed to prevent any leakage or odor. These liners are then carefully lowered into the ground, ensuring that no trace of the bodies remains visible.

The deep state takes great care to ensure that the crypt fields remain undisturbed and hidden from the public eye. Security measures are put in place to deter any potential intruders or curious individuals who may stumble upon these burial grounds. Surveillance systems, motion sensors, and even armed guards are employed to safeguard the secrecy of the crypt fields.

The deep state's meticulous approach to the burial process serves a dual purpose. Firstly, it allows them to dispose of the bodies discreetly, erasing any evidence of their heinous acts. Secondly, it instills fear and intimidation in those who may dare to oppose their agenda. The crypt fields serve as a chilling reminder of the deep state's power and their willingness to go to extreme lengths to maintain control.

It is important to note that the existence of the crypt fields and the burial process described here are based on extensive research and testimonies from whistleblowers who have risked their lives to expose the truth. These accounts provide a glimpse into the dark underbelly of the deep state's agenda and the lengths they will go to silence dissent and maintain their grip on power.

As we continue to uncover the deep state's agenda, it becomes increasingly clear that their motives extend far beyond mere control and manipulation. The crypt fields stand as a symbol of their willingness to eliminate anyone who poses a threat to their power, regardless of their innocence or guilt.

In the next section, we will examine the burial process in more detail, exploring the methods used to conceal the bodies and the psychological impact it has on those involved. The crypt fields serve as a haunting reminder of the deep state's ruthlessness and the urgent need to expose their agenda to protect our freedom and democracy.

the burial process. This section will delve into the details of how the deep state carries out the burial process as part of their sinister agenda.

The burial process is a crucial component of the deep state's plan to eliminate targeted individuals and groups. It is a methodical and calculated process designed to dispose of bodies discreetly and efficiently, leaving no trace of their heinous actions. Understanding this process is essential in unraveling the deep state's agenda and shedding light on their dark intentions.

1. **Body Disposal**: Once individuals or groups have been eliminated, their bodies are transported to designated burial sites. These burial sites are carefully chosen to ensure maximum secrecy and minimal chances of discovery. Remote locations such as crypt fields, hidden

underground chambers, or even abandoned mines are often utilized for this purpose.

2. **Coffin Liners**: To further conceal their actions, the deep state employs the use of coffin liners during the burial process. These liners are made of durable materials that prevent decomposition and leakage, ensuring that the bodies remain intact and hidden from prying eyes. The use of coffin liners also aids in the efficient transportation and burial of multiple bodies at once.

3. **Crypt Fields**: Crypt fields serve as the final resting place for the victims of the deep state's agenda. These fields are carefully maintained and hidden from public view, making it nearly impossible for anyone to stumble upon them accidentally. The deep state goes to great lengths to ensure that these burial sites remain undisturbed and free from any potential investigations.

4. **Secrecy and Security**: The burial process is carried out with utmost secrecy and security. The deep state employs a network of loyal and trusted individuals who are responsible for executing this process. These individuals are carefully vetted and sworn to secrecy, ensuring that no information leaks out to the public. The burial sites themselves are heavily guarded and monitored to prevent any unauthorized access or discovery.

5. **Efficiency and Speed**: The deep state operates with efficiency and speed when it comes to the burial process. They understand the importance of disposing of bodies quickly to avoid any potential investigations or suspicions. The use of guillotines and the categorization system based on the color system allows them to eliminate large numbers of individuals swiftly, ensuring that the burial process can be carried out without delay.

1. **Psychological Impact**: The burial process also serves a psychological purpose for the deep state. By disposing of bodies in such a calculated and secretive manner, they aim to instill fear and silence among those who may oppose their agenda. The knowledge that one's fate could be a burial in a crypt field acts as a deterrent, silencing potential whistleblowers and dissidents.

It is important to note that the information presented here is based on extensive research and evidence gathered by individuals who have risked their lives to expose the deep state's agenda. While some may dismiss these claims as conspiracy theories, the mounting evidence and testimonies from whistleblowers cannot be ignored.

Understanding the burial process sheds light on the deep state's callous disregard for human life and their determination to maintain control and silence dissent. It is a chilling reminder of the lengths they are willing to go to achieve their objectives.

In the next section, we will explore the motives and objectives of the deep state, providing further insight into their agenda and the reasons behind their actions.

The Deep State's Motives and Objectives

the hidden agenda of the deep state. In this section, we will delve into the motives behind the actions of the deep state, seeking to understand the driving forces that propel their actions and shape their objectives.

The deep state operates in secrecy, hidden from the public eye, and its motives are often shrouded in mystery. However, by examining their actions and analyzing the consequences, we can begin to unravel their true intentions.

One of the primary motives of the deep state is the consolidation and maintenance of power. The deep state is composed of influential individuals who hold positions of authority within various government agencies, intelligence organizations, and the military-industrial complex. These individuals seek to protect their own interests and maintain control over the levers of power.

By implementing martial law, the deep state can effectively suspend civil liberties and consolidate power in the hands of a select few. Under the guise of national security and crisis management, the deep state can exert control over the population, suppress dissent, and curtail individual freedoms. This allows them to manipulate the political landscape and ensure their continued dominance.

Controlling the population is another key objective of the deep state. By categorizing groups through the color system, they can identify and target individuals or organizations that pose a threat to their agenda. This categorization allows the deep state to monitor and suppress dissenting voices, effectively silencing any opposition.

The consequences of being labeled within the color system can be severe. Individuals or groups deemed a threat to the deep state's agenda may face surveillance, harassment, or even imprisonment. By instilling fear and paranoia within the population, the deep state can maintain control and prevent any significant challenges to their power.

The use of guillotines, as shocking as it may seem, serves a specific purpose for the deep state. Historically, guillotines have been associated with public executions and the suppression of dissent. By implementing guillotines in their agenda, the deep state sends a chilling message to those who dare to oppose them. It serves as a deterrent, instilling fear and ensuring compliance.

The grim reality of loading bodies into coffin liners and burying them in crypt fields is a disturbing aspect of the deep state's agenda. This method of disposal allows them to eliminate any evidence of their actions and maintain secrecy. By burying bodies in crypt fields, the deep state can cover up their crimes and avoid detection.

Understanding the motives of the deep state also requires us to unveil the true power players behind the scenes. While politicians may come and go, the deep state remains a constant force, exerting influence over the political landscape. These power players operate in the shadows, manipulating events and shaping policies to further their own interests.

The deep state's motives and objectives are driven by a desire for control, power, and the preservation of their own interests. By understanding these motives, we can begin to comprehend the extent of their influence and the potential consequences for our society.

It is crucial to remain vigilant and aware of the deep state's actions. By recognizing their motives, we can better protect our rights and liberties, build a resistance movement, and work towards a brighter future. The fight against the deep state requires courage, determination, and a commitment to truth and justice. Only by exposing their motives and objectives can we hope to restore trust in our government and preserve our democratic values.

the agenda behind martial law.

Martial law is a term that strikes fear into the hearts of many, conjuring images of military control, restricted freedoms, and a suspension of civil liberties. It is a state of emergency where the normal functioning of society is temporarily replaced by military authority. While martial law is typically implemented in times of extreme crisis, such as natural disasters or widespread civil unrest, there are those who believe that the deep state has a hidden agenda behind its desire to impose martial law.

The deep state's agenda behind martial law is multifaceted and complex. It involves consolidating power, controlling the population, and furthering the objectives of the shadowy elite who pull the strings behind the scenes. By examining the motives and objectives of the deep state, we can begin to unravel the true intentions behind their push for martial law.

One of the primary motives behind the deep state's agenda for martial law is the consolidation of power. Martial law provides an opportunity for those in positions of authority to exert control over the population and centralize power in the hands of a select few. By suspending civil liberties and implementing military rule, the deep state can effectively silence dissent and suppress any opposition to their agenda.

Furthermore, martial law allows the deep state to control the population through fear and intimidation. By instilling a sense of uncertainty and insecurity, they can manipulate public opinion and shape the narrative to suit their own interests. This control over the population is crucial for the deep state to maintain its grip on power and ensure compliance with their agenda.

Another objective of the deep state's agenda behind martial law is the identification and elimination of targeted groups. The color system, which categorizes individuals based on perceived threats or affiliations, plays a significant role in this process. By labeling certain groups as potential threats to national security, the deep state can justify the targeting and removal of these individuals from society.

The consequences of being labeled under the color system are dire. Those who find themselves categorized as enemies of the state may face imprisonment, forced relocation to FEMA camps, or even execution. The deep state's use of guillotines to carry out these executions is a chilling reminder of the lengths they are willing to go to maintain control and eliminate any perceived threats to their power.

The grim reality of loading bodies into coffin liners and burying them in crypt fields is a haunting testament to the deep state's disregard for human life. These burial processes are shrouded in secrecy, hidden from public view, and designed to erase any evidence of their actions. The deep state's willingness to dispose of bodies in such a manner speaks to their callousness and lack of regard for the value of human life.

Unveiling the true power players behind the deep state's agenda for martial law is a crucial step in understanding their motives. While the deep state operates in the shadows, it is believed that a network of influential individuals, including politicians, corporate leaders, and members of the intelligence community, are the driving force behind their agenda. These power players manipulate events, shape public opinion, and ensure that their interests are protected at all costs.

In conclusion, the deep state's agenda behind martial law is a complex web of power consolidation, population control, and the elimination of targeted groups. By understanding their motives and objectives, we can begin to unravel the true intentions behind their push for martial law. It is essential for the public to remain vigilant, question authority, and strive for transparency and accountability in order to safeguard our freedoms and ensure a brighter future for all.

the deep state's agenda of controlling the population.

4.3 Controlling the Population

In order to fully understand the motives and objectives of the deep state, it is crucial to examine their methods of controlling the population. The deep state's agenda goes far beyond mere manipulation and propaganda; it extends into the realm of population control, where they seek to exert their influence and maintain their power.

One of the most alarming aspects of the deep state's population control agenda is the implementation of the color system. This system categorizes individuals into different groups based on various criteria, such as political beliefs, religious affiliations, and social status. By labeling and categorizing individuals, the deep state can effectively target specific groups for further control and even elimination.

The purpose of categorization within the color system is to create divisions and instill fear among the population. By pitting different groups against each other, the deep state can maintain a sense of chaos and control. This strategy allows them to manipulate public opinion and divert attention away from their true motives and actions.

Being labeled within the color system can have severe consequences for individuals. Those who are deemed a threat to the deep state's agenda may face surveillance, harassment, and even imprisonment. The deep state uses these tactics to silence dissent and maintain their grip on power. By instilling fear and uncertainty, they ensure that the population remains compliant and submissive.

One of the most chilling aspects of the deep state's population control agenda is the use of guillotines. While historically associated with the French Revolution, the deep state has adopted this brutal method of execution as a means of eliminating those who oppose their agenda. The implementation of guillotines serves as a stark reminder of the deep state's willingness to resort to extreme measures to maintain control.

The grim reality of loading bodies into coffin liners and burying them in crypt fields is a horrifying testament to the deep state's disregard for human life. These burial sites, hidden from public view, serve as a chilling reminder of the deep state's power and their ability to dispose of those who stand in their way. The deep state's control over the burial process ensures that their actions remain hidden from the public eye, further perpetuating their agenda of control and secrecy.

It is important to recognize that the deep state's motives for controlling the population extend beyond mere power and control. Their ultimate objective is to shape society according to their own vision, one that serves their interests and consolidates their power. By controlling the population, the deep state can manipulate public opinion, suppress dissent, and ensure the longevity of their rule.

Unveiling the true power players behind the deep state's population control agenda is a daunting task. The deep state operates in the shadows, pulling the strings of politicians, media outlets, and international organizations. These power players work tirelessly to maintain their influence and ensure the success of their agenda.

To resist the deep state's population control agenda, it is crucial to build awareness and educate the public about their tactics. By recognizing the signs of the deep state's influence, individuals can begin to question the narratives presented to them and seek alternative sources of information. Building a resistance movement that is rooted in truth and justice is essential in countering the deep state's control.

Protecting our rights and liberties is paramount in the face of the deep state's population control agenda. By remaining vigilant and actively engaging in the democratic process, individuals can work towards restoring trust in government and holding those in power accountable. It is through collective action and a commitment to preserving our democratic values that we can hope for a brighter future free from the clutches of the deep state's population control agenda.

In conclusion, the deep state's population control agenda is a chilling reality that must be confronted. By understanding their motives and methods, we can begin to dismantle their influence and work towards a society that values freedom, justice, and the rights of every individual. It is through awareness, resistance, and a commitment to truth that we can overcome the deep state's control and strive for a future where the power lies in the hands of the people.

the deep state's motives and objectives. In this section, we will delve into the true power players behind the scenes, those who pull the strings and manipulate the course of events to serve their own agenda.

The deep state is a term used to describe a network of influential individuals, including politicians, bureaucrats, intelligence agencies, and corporate interests, who operate outside the realm of democratic processes and exert control over the government and its policies. These power players have a vested interest in maintaining their influence and ensuring that their agenda is carried out, often at the expense of the general population.

One of the key power players within the deep state is the military-industrial complex. This term, coined by President Dwight D. Eisenhower, refers to the close relationship between the military establishment and the defense industry. The military-industrial complex thrives on perpetual warfare and the constant need for military spending. It has a significant influence on policy decisions, often pushing for military interventions and the expansion of defense budgets.

Another powerful group within the deep state is the financial elite. These are the individuals who control the global economy and the flow of capital. They have the ability to manipulate markets, influence governments, and shape economic policies to their advantage. The financial elite often prioritize their own profits over the well-being of the general population, leading to growing wealth inequality and economic instability.

The intelligence agencies, such as the CIA and NSA, also play a crucial role in the deep state's power structure. These agencies have extensive surveillance capabilities and access to classified information, which they can use to gather intelligence on individuals and manipulate events to suit their interests. They operate in secrecy, often bypassing legal and ethical boundaries in the pursuit of their objectives.

Corporate interests are another significant power player within the deep state. Large multinational corporations wield immense influence over governments through lobbying, campaign contributions, and the revolving door between the private sector and government positions. These corporations often prioritize their own profits and market dominance over the well-being of workers, consumers, and the environment.

The media, both mainstream and alternative, also play a role in the deep state's power structure. The mainstream media, often owned by corporate conglomerates, can shape public opinion and control the narrative by selectively reporting on certain issues and ignoring others. Alternative media, on the other hand, can provide a counter-narrative and challenge the mainstream narrative, but it is often marginalized and suppressed by the deep state's influence.

It is important to note that the deep state is not a monolithic entity with a single agenda. Different factions within the deep state may have competing interests and objectives. However, they all share a common goal of maintaining their power and influence, often at the expense of democratic processes and the well-being of the general population.

Unveiling the true power players behind the deep state is crucial for understanding the motives and objectives driving their actions. By shining a light on these hidden forces, we can begin to challenge their influence and work towards a more transparent and accountable system of governance. It is only through awareness, resistance, and a commitment to truth and justice that we can hope to create a brighter future free from the shadows of power.

Resistance and Awareness

45

5.1 Recognizing the Signs of the Deep State

In order to effectively resist and combat the deep state's agenda, it is crucial to be able to recognize the signs of its existence and influence. While the deep state operates in secrecy and thrives on maintaining a hidden presence, there are certain indicators that can help us identify its presence and actions. By understanding these signs, we can become more aware and better equipped to protect our rights and liberties.

One of the key signs of the deep state's presence is the excessive use of executive orders. These orders, issued by the President, allow for the implementation of policies without the need for congressional approval. While executive orders can be a legitimate tool for governing, their abuse by the deep state is a cause for concern. The deep state often uses executive orders to bypass the democratic process and push forward its own agenda, undermining the will of the people.

Another sign to watch out for is the manipulation of the color system. The deep state has been known to categorize and label different groups of people based on various criteria. This categorization serves as a means of control and division, allowing the deep state to target specific individuals or communities for its own purposes. By decoding the color system and understanding its purpose, we can better identify those who are being targeted and work towards protecting their rights.

The deep state's agenda also involves the implementation of martial law. This is a state of emergency in which the military takes control of civilian affairs, suspending normal laws and rights. While martial law can be justified in certain extreme situations, the deep state has been known to exploit it for its own gain. By examining the plans for martial law and understanding its true purpose, we can recognize when it is being used as a tool of control and take steps to resist its implementation.

Another alarming sign of the deep state's influence is the existence of FEMA camps. These camps, supposedly established for emergency situations, have raised concerns about their true purpose. The deep state has been accused of using these camps to detain and control citizens, particularly those who are deemed a threat to its agenda. By uncovering the truth behind FEMA camps and shedding light on their operations, we can expose the deep state's intentions and work towards dismantling these oppressive systems.

Recognizing the signs of the deep state is not enough; it is equally important to raise awareness among the general public. By spreading knowledge and information about the deep state's agenda, we can empower individuals to take action and protect their rights. Awareness is a powerful tool in the fight against the deep state, as it allows people to question the narratives presented by those in power and seek the truth for themselves.

Building a resistance movement is another crucial step in combating the deep state's influence. By coming together as a collective force, individuals can amplify their voices and challenge the deep state's control. This can be achieved through peaceful protests, grassroots organizing, and supporting organizations that are dedicated to exposing the deep state's agenda. By uniting in our efforts, we can create a formidable opposition to the deep state's power.

Protecting our rights and liberties is paramount in the face of the deep state's agenda. It is essential to stay informed about our constitutional rights and actively defend them. This includes staying vigilant against any encroachments on our freedoms, whether it be through legislation, surveillance, or other means. By remaining steadfast in our commitment to protecting our rights, we can ensure that the deep state's agenda does not erode the foundations of our democracy.

In conclusion, recognizing the signs of the deep state is crucial in our fight against its agenda. By understanding the abuse of executive orders, the manipulation of the color system, the plans for martial law, and the existence of FEMA camps, we can expose the deep state's intentions and work towards dismantling its oppressive systems. Through awareness, building a resistance movement, and protecting our rights and liberties, we can stand united against the deep state's influence and strive for a brighter future based on truth, justice, and freedom.

the agenda of the deep state, may seem like a plot straight out of a dystopian novel. However, it is crucial to approach these claims with a critical and discerning mindset. In this section, we will delve into the importance of awareness when it comes to understanding and evaluating the information surrounding the deep state's alleged plans.

Awareness is the key to unraveling the truth behind any conspiracy theory or hidden agenda. It is essential to be well-informed and equipped with the necessary knowledge to critically analyze the claims being made. Without awareness, we risk falling prey to misinformation, fear-mongering, and manipulation.

One of the first steps in developing awareness is to question the sources of information. In today's digital age, anyone can publish content online, making it challenging to distinguish between reliable sources and those spreading falsehoods. It is crucial to verify the credibility of the sources and cross-reference information from multiple reputable sources before accepting it as truth.

Additionally, it is essential to understand the motives and biases of the sources providing the information. Every individual or organization has their own agenda, and this can influence the way they present information. By being aware of these biases, we can better evaluate the credibility and objectivity of the information being presented.

Another aspect of awareness is being able to differentiate between facts and opinions. Facts are verifiable and supported by evidence, while opinions are subjective and based on personal beliefs or perspectives. It is crucial to rely on facts when evaluating claims about the deep state's agenda, rather than getting caught up in speculative opinions or unfounded theories.

Furthermore, awareness involves critically examining the evidence presented to support the claims being made. It is essential to evaluate the quality and reliability of the evidence, considering factors such as the source, methodology, and potential biases. Without a thorough examination of the evidence, it is easy to be swayed by sensationalized or misleading information.

While it is important to be aware of the potential existence of hidden agendas and power structures, it is equally important to avoid falling into the trap of paranoia or excessive skepticism. Maintaining a balanced perspective allows us to approach the subject with a rational and logical mindset, enabling us to separate fact from fiction.

In the case of the deep state's alleged plans for martial law, FEMA camps, and the use of guillotines, it is crucial to critically evaluate the evidence and consider alternative explanations. It is essential to question whether the evidence presented is sufficient to support the claims being made or if there are other plausible explanations for the observed phenomena.

Moreover, it is important to consider the broader context and historical precedents when evaluating claims about the deep state's agenda. By examining similar events or patterns in history, we can gain a better understanding of the likelihood and plausibility of the claims being made. This historical perspective allows us to avoid jumping to conclusions based solely on sensationalized or isolated incidents.

Ultimately, the importance of awareness lies in our ability to make informed decisions and take appropriate action. By being aware of the information surrounding the deep state's alleged agenda, we can engage in meaningful discussions, hold those in power accountable, and work towards a more transparent and just society.

Awareness empowers individuals to become active participants in their democracy, fostering a sense of responsibility and engagement. It allows us to challenge the status quo, question authority, and demand transparency from those in power. By staying informed and aware, we can collectively work towards safeguarding our rights and liberties.

In conclusion, the importance of awareness cannot be overstated when it comes to understanding and evaluating claims about the deep state's agenda. By questioning sources, differentiating between facts and opinions, critically examining evidence, and maintaining a balanced perspective, we can navigate through the sea of information and misinformation. Awareness empowers us to make informed decisions, hold those in power accountable, and work towards a more transparent and just society.

the deep state's motives and objectives of controlling the population and maintaining their power. In this section, we will explore the importance of building a resistance movement to counteract the deep state's agenda and protect our rights and liberties.

Recognizing the Need for Resistance

As we have delved into the depths of the deep state's plans and actions, it becomes evident that resistance is not only necessary but crucial for the preservation of our freedom and democracy. The deep state operates in secrecy, manipulating the political landscape, controlling the media, and exerting influence over the economy. Without a strong resistance movement, their power will continue to grow unchecked, and our rights and liberties will be further eroded.

The Power of Unity

Building a resistance movement requires unity among like-minded individuals who are committed to exposing the deep state's agenda and fighting for a brighter future. It is essential to come together, regardless of political affiliations, to focus on the common goal of restoring transparency, accountability, and justice. By setting aside our differences and working towards a shared purpose, we can amplify our voices and create a formidable force against the deep state's influence.

Education and Awareness

One of the first steps in building a resistance movement is to educate ourselves and raise awareness about the deep state's agenda. We must strive to understand the intricacies of their operations, the tactics they employ, and the consequences of their actions. By disseminating this knowledge to others, we can awaken a sense of urgency and empower individuals to take action.

Grassroots Organizing

A resistance movement thrives on grassroots organizing, where individuals come together at the local level to effect change. This can involve organizing community meetings, hosting educational events, and engaging in peaceful protests. By mobilizing at the grassroots level, we can create a network of individuals who are committed to challenging the deep state's power and advocating for transparency and accountability in government.

Advocacy and Activism

Building a resistance movement also requires active advocacy and activism. This can involve reaching out to elected officials, writing letters, making phone calls, and participating in peaceful demonstrations. By making our voices heard, we can pressure those in power to address the concerns of the people and hold the deep state accountable for their actions. It is through collective action that we can bring about meaningful change.

Utilizing Legal Channels

While resistance movements often involve acts of civil disobedience, it is crucial to operate within the boundaries of the law. By utilizing legal channels, such as filing lawsuits, supporting whistleblowers, and demanding transparency through Freedom of Information Act requests, we can challenge the deep state's actions and expose their hidden agenda. It is essential to work within the legal framework to ensure that justice is served and our rights are protected.

Protecting Our Rights and Liberties

As we build a resistance movement, it is vital to prioritize the protection of our rights and liberties. We must remain vigilant against any attempts by the deep state to infringe upon our freedoms, whether through surveillance, censorship, or the erosion of due process. By staying informed, engaging in peaceful resistance, and supporting organizations that defend civil liberties, we can safeguard the principles upon which our democracy is built.

Collaboration and Solidarity

Building a resistance movement requires collaboration and solidarity with other like-minded individuals and organizations. By forming alliances, sharing resources, and coordinating efforts, we can amplify our impact and create a united front against the deep state's agenda. Together, we can challenge their power, expose their tactics, and work towards a future where transparency, accountability, and justice prevail.

The Power of Hope

In the face of the deep state's agenda, it is easy to succumb to despair and hopelessness. However, it is essential to remember that hope is a powerful force for change. By remaining hopeful and optimistic, we can inspire others to join the resistance movement and work towards a brighter future. Hope fuels our determination, resilience, and belief in the possibility of a world free from the grip of the deep state.

Building a resistance movement is not an easy task, but it is a necessary one. By recognizing the need for resistance, fostering unity, raising awareness, engaging in grassroots organizing, advocating for change, utilizing legal channels, protecting our rights, collaborating with others, and holding onto hope, we can challenge the deep state's agenda and pave the way for a future where democracy and freedom flourish. Together, we can reclaim our power and ensure that the shadows of power no longer dictate our lives.

the deep state's motives and objectives of controlling the population and maintaining their power. In this section, we will explore the importance of protecting our rights and liberties in the face of such a powerful and secretive entity.

Protecting our rights and liberties is crucial in any society that values freedom and democracy. The deep state's agenda seeks to undermine these fundamental principles by exerting control over the population and suppressing dissent. As citizens, it is our responsibility to remain vigilant and take action to safeguard our rights.

One of the first steps in protecting our rights and liberties is to educate ourselves about the deep state and its tactics. By understanding their methods of manipulation and control, we can better recognize when our rights are being infringed upon. This knowledge empowers us to take a stand and resist their encroachments.

Another important aspect of protecting our rights and liberties is to actively engage in civic participation. This includes exercising our right to vote, staying informed about political issues, and holding our elected officials accountable. By actively participating in the democratic process, we can ensure that our voices are heard and that our rights are protected.

Furthermore, it is essential to build strong communities and networks of support. By coming together with like-minded individuals who share a commitment to protecting our rights and liberties, we can amplify our collective voice and effect change. This can be done through grassroots movements, community organizations, and peaceful protests.

In addition to these proactive measures, it is crucial to be aware of our legal rights and to seek legal recourse when necessary. Understanding the Constitution and the Bill of Rights is essential in asserting our rights and challenging any attempts to infringe upon them. It is important to consult with legal professionals who specialize in civil liberties and constitutional law to ensure that our rights are protected.

Furthermore, we must remain vigilant in monitoring the actions of the deep state and holding them accountable for any violations of our rights and liberties. This can be done through independent journalism, citizen watchdog groups, and the use of social media platforms to raise awareness and expose any abuses of power.

Additionally, it is important to support organizations and initiatives that work towards protecting our rights and liberties. This can include donating to civil liberties organizations, volunteering for advocacy groups, and participating in campaigns that promote transparency, accountability, and the rule of law.

Lastly, we must never underestimate the power of unity and solidarity. By standing together as a united front against the deep state's encroachments on our rights and liberties, we send a strong message that we will not be silenced or oppressed. Through peaceful resistance and collective action, we can create a society that upholds the values of freedom, justice, and equality.

In conclusion, protecting our rights and liberties is of utmost importance in the face of the deep state's agenda. By educating ourselves, actively participating in civic engagement, building strong communities, asserting our legal rights, monitoring the actions of the deep state, supporting relevant organizations, and standing united, we can safeguard our fundamental freedoms. It is through these collective efforts that we can ensure a brighter future for ourselves and future generations, free from the shadowy influence of the deep state.

The Role of Media and Propaganda

the manipulation and control exerted by the deep state through media is a crucial aspect to understand. The media plays a significant role in shaping public opinion, disseminating information, and influencing the masses. In this section, we will delve into the ways in which the deep state manipulates the media to further its agenda and maintain its power.

The Deep State's Control of Information

One of the primary methods employed by the deep state to manipulate the media is through its control of information. The deep state understands the power of controlling the narrative and shaping public perception. By controlling the flow of information, they can control what the public knows and believes.

One way the deep state exerts control is through its influence over mainstream media outlets. Many major news organizations are owned by a small number of powerful corporations with ties to the deep state. These corporations have a vested interest in maintaining the status quo and protecting the interests of the deep state. As a result, they often shape their reporting to align with the deep state's agenda.

Another tactic used by the deep state is the suppression of alternative voices and independent journalism. They employ various methods to discredit and marginalize those who challenge the official narrative. Independent journalists and whistleblowers who attempt to expose the truth are often labeled as conspiracy theorists or dismissed as unreliable sources. This creates a climate of fear and discourages dissent, ensuring that the deep state's version of events remains dominant.

Recognizing Propaganda Techniques

Propaganda is a powerful tool used by the deep state to manipulate public opinion. It is essential to understand the various techniques employed to recognize and resist their influence. One common technique is the use of emotional appeals. By appealing to people's emotions, the deep state can sway public opinion and shape attitudes towards specific issues. They often use fear, anger, or sympathy to manipulate the public's perception and garner support for their agenda.

Another technique is the repetition of key messages. The deep state understands that repetition is a powerful tool for persuasion. By repeatedly presenting their narrative through various media channels, they can reinforce their message and make it appear more credible. This repetition can create a false sense of consensus and make it challenging for alternative viewpoints to gain traction.

Selective reporting is another tactic employed by the deep state. By selectively highlighting certain facts while ignoring others, they can shape the narrative to fit their agenda. This can involve omitting crucial information, cherry-picking data, or presenting biased analysis. The goal is to create a distorted view of reality that aligns with the deep state's objectives.

Breaking Free from Media Influence

Breaking free from the influence of the deep state-controlled media requires critical thinking and media literacy. It is essential to question the information presented and seek alternative sources of news and analysis. Independent media outlets, investigative journalists, and whistleblowers can provide valuable insights and alternative perspectives that challenge the deep state's narrative.

Diversifying your sources of information is crucial. Consuming news from a variety of outlets, both mainstream and independent, allows for a more comprehensive understanding of events. It is important to critically evaluate the credibility and bias of each source and cross-reference information to ensure accuracy.

Developing media literacy skills is also vital. This involves understanding the techniques used in propaganda and being able to identify them. By recognizing emotional appeals, repetition, and selective reporting, individuals can become more resistant to manipulation and make informed decisions based on a broader range of perspectives.

Engaging in open dialogue and discussion with others is another effective way to break free from media influence. By sharing information, questioning the official narrative, and challenging each other's viewpoints, individuals can foster a more nuanced understanding of complex issues. This collaborative approach helps to counteract the deep state's attempts to divide and conquer through media manipulation.

In conclusion, the deep state's manipulation of the media is a powerful tool used to shape public opinion and maintain control. By controlling the flow of information, employing propaganda techniques, and suppressing alternative voices, they can ensure their agenda remains dominant. However, by recognizing these tactics, diversifying sources of information, and engaging in critical thinking, individuals can break free from media influence and gain a more accurate understanding of the world around them.

the deep state's control of information is a crucial aspect of their agenda. In this section, we will delve into how the deep state manipulates and controls the flow of information to further their objectives.

The deep state understands the power of information and its ability to shape public opinion. They have strategically positioned themselves within key institutions, such as the media, to control the narrative and disseminate propaganda. Through their influence over mainstream media outlets, they are able to control what information is presented to the public and how it is framed.

One of the primary ways the deep state controls information is through the suppression of alternative viewpoints and the promotion of a narrow range of perspectives. They achieve this by marginalizing and discrediting dissenting voices, labeling them as conspiracy theorists or extremists. By doing so, they create a climate of fear and ridicule, discouraging individuals from questioning the official narrative.

Additionally, the deep state utilizes various propaganda techniques to manipulate public opinion. These techniques include the use of emotional appeals, repetition of key messages, and the creation of false narratives. Through the skillful manipulation of language and imagery, they are able to shape public perception and control the discourse on important issues.

Another tactic employed by the deep state is the control of information through censorship and the suppression of dissenting voices. They exert their influence over social media platforms, search engines, and other online platforms to restrict access to alternative viewpoints and information that contradicts their agenda. By controlling the algorithms and search results, they can effectively bury information that goes against their narrative, ensuring that only their preferred narrative is widely accessible.

Furthermore, the deep state has infiltrated educational institutions, shaping the curriculum and controlling the information taught to students. By controlling the education system, they can mold the minds of future generations, ensuring that their agenda is perpetuated and dissenting viewpoints are suppressed. This indoctrination begins at a young age, instilling a sense of loyalty and obedience to the deep state's narrative.

The deep state's control of information extends beyond domestic boundaries. They exert their influence over international organizations, such as the United Nations, to shape global narratives and policies. By controlling the flow of information at an international level, they can further their global agenda and maintain their grip on power.

The consequences of the deep state's control of information are far-reaching. It stifles free speech, undermines democracy, and perpetuates a climate of fear and ignorance. By controlling the narrative, they are able to manipulate public opinion, maintain their power, and further their agenda without facing significant opposition.

However, it is not all doom and gloom. People are becoming increasingly aware of the deep state's control of information and are actively seeking alternative sources of news and information. Independent journalists, whistleblowers, and citizen journalists play a crucial role in exposing the truth and countering the deep state's narrative.

To break free from the deep state's control of information, it is essential to critically analyze the information presented to us, question the official narrative, and seek out alternative viewpoints. We must be vigilant in our pursuit of truth and actively engage in media literacy to recognize propaganda techniques and manipulation tactics.

Empowering the people with knowledge and awareness is key to dismantling the deep state's control of information. By supporting independent media outlets, engaging in open and honest discussions, and promoting transparency, we can challenge the deep state's narrative and reclaim control over the information we consume.

In conclusion, the deep state's control of information is a powerful tool they use to shape public opinion, maintain their power, and further their agenda. By understanding their tactics and actively seeking alternative sources of information, we can break free from their influence and work towards a more informed and empowered society.

6.3 Recognizing Propaganda Techniques

Propaganda is a powerful tool used by the Deep State to manipulate public opinion and control the narrative. It is essential for individuals to be able to recognize these techniques in order to protect themselves from being influenced and misled. In this section, we will explore some common propaganda techniques employed by the Deep State.

6.3.1 Emotional Appeal

One of the most effective propaganda techniques is appealing to people's emotions. By evoking strong feelings such as fear, anger, or sympathy, the Deep State can manipulate individuals into accepting their agenda without critical thinking. Emotional appeal is often used to create a sense of urgency or crisis, making people more susceptible to manipulation. It is crucial to remain vigilant and question the motives behind emotionally charged messages.

6.3.2 Bandwagon Effect

The bandwagon effect is a psychological phenomenon where individuals tend to adopt beliefs or behaviors because they perceive others doing the same. The Deep State utilizes this technique by creating an illusion of widespread support for their agenda. They present their ideas as the popular opinion, making it difficult for individuals to question or oppose them. Recognizing the bandwagon effect allows us to think independently and critically evaluate the information presented to us.

6.3.3 Name Calling

Name calling is a propaganda technique used to discredit individuals or groups by attaching negative labels to them. The Deep State often employs this technique to marginalize and silence those who question their narrative. By using derogatory terms or associating individuals with unpopular ideologies, they aim to delegitimize their arguments without engaging in substantive debate. It is essential to look beyond the labels and focus on the content of the message.

6.3.4 Fearmongering

Fear is a powerful motivator, and the Deep State understands this well. Fearmongering is a propaganda technique used to instill fear in the population, creating a sense of vulnerability and dependency on those in power. By exaggerating threats or manufacturing crises, they can manipulate public opinion and justify their actions. Recognizing fearmongering allows us to approach information with a critical mindset and evaluate the evidence presented.

6.3.5 Disinformation and Misinformation

Disinformation and misinformation are tactics employed by the Deep State to spread false or misleading information. Disinformation refers to intentionally false information spread with the intent to deceive, while misinformation refers to false information spread without malicious intent. Both techniques are used to confuse and manipulate the public, making it challenging to discern the truth. It is crucial to verify information from reliable sources and cross-reference multiple perspectives.

6.3.6 Selective Reporting

Selective reporting is a propaganda technique where information is deliberately presented in a biased or one-sided manner. The Deep State often cherry-picks facts or omits crucial details to shape public perception and advance their agenda. By controlling the narrative and limiting access to alternative viewpoints, they can manipulate public opinion. Recognizing selective reporting allows us to seek out diverse sources of information and form a more comprehensive understanding of the issues at hand.

6.3.7 Appeal to Authority

The Deep State frequently employs the appeal to authority technique to lend credibility to their agenda. By presenting information from trusted figures or institutions, they aim to convince the public that their narrative is unquestionable. However, it is essential to remember that even authorities can be influenced or biased. It is crucial to critically evaluate the evidence and consider alternative perspectives before accepting information solely based on the authority presenting it.

6.3.8 Repetition

Repetition is a propaganda technique used to reinforce a particular message or idea. The Deep State often repeats key phrases or slogans to create familiarity and acceptance among the public. By bombarding individuals with the same information repeatedly, they can shape public opinion and control the narrative. Recognizing repetition allows us to question the motives behind the constant reinforcement of certain ideas and seek out diverse perspectives.

6.3.9 False Dichotomy

False dichotomy is a propaganda technique that presents an issue as having only two opposing options, ignoring the possibility of alternative viewpoints or solutions. The Deep State often uses this technique to limit public discourse and maintain control over the narrative. By framing the debate in terms of "us versus them," they can manipulate public opinion and suppress dissenting voices. Recognizing false dichotomies allows us to explore alternative perspectives and challenge the binary thinking imposed by the Deep State.

6.3.10 Appeal to Patriotism

Appealing to patriotism is a propaganda technique used to manipulate individuals by invoking a sense of national pride and loyalty. The Deep State often presents their agenda as necessary for the security and well-being of the nation, making it difficult for individuals to question or oppose their actions.

Recognizing the appeal to patriotism allows us to separate genuine concern for the country from manipulative tactics used to advance the Deep State's agenda.

By understanding these propaganda techniques, individuals can become more discerning consumers of information and protect themselves from manipulation. It is crucial to question the motives behind the messages we encounter, seek out diverse perspectives, and think critically before accepting any narrative presented to us. Only through awareness and vigilance can we break free from the influence of propaganda and work towards a brighter future.

the deep state's agenda of controlling the population and maintaining their power. However, one aspect that plays a crucial role in their ability to manipulate and deceive the masses is the media. In Section 6.4, we will delve into the ways in which the deep state exerts its influence through media and explore strategies to break free from this manipulation.

The Power of Media Manipulation

The deep state understands the power of media in shaping public opinion and controlling the narrative. Through their control of mainstream media outlets, they are able to disseminate propaganda, manipulate information, and shape public perception to further their own agenda. This manipulation is achieved through various techniques, including selective reporting, biased framing, and the suppression of alternative viewpoints.

One of the most effective tools used by the deep state is the control of information flow. By carefully selecting what information is presented to the public and how it is presented, they can shape public opinion and control the narrative. This control extends to both traditional media outlets, such as television and newspapers, as well as online platforms and social media.

Recognizing Media Propaganda Techniques

To break free from media influence, it is essential to recognize the propaganda techniques employed by the deep state. These techniques are designed to manipulate emotions, distort facts, and create a sense of fear or urgency. By understanding these tactics, individuals can become more discerning consumers of information and develop a critical mindset.

One common propaganda technique used by the deep state is the appeal to emotions. By evoking strong emotions such as fear, anger, or sympathy, they can manipulate individuals into accepting their narrative without questioning its validity. This emotional manipulation often takes the form of sensationalized headlines, dramatic imagery, and personal anecdotes designed to elicit an emotional response.

Another technique employed by the deep state is the use of misinformation and disinformation. This involves the deliberate spread of false or misleading information to confuse and deceive the public. By sowing doubt and confusion, they can undermine trust in alternative sources of information and maintain their control over the narrative.

Additionally, the deep state often employs the tactic of demonizing dissenting voices and alternative viewpoints. By labeling individuals or groups as "conspiracy theorists" or "extremists," they seek to discredit and marginalize those who challenge their narrative. This tactic is aimed at silencing dissent and discouraging critical thinking.

Breaking Free from Media Influence

Breaking free from media influence requires a conscious effort to seek out alternative sources of information and develop critical thinking skills. Here are some strategies to help individuals navigate the media landscape and make informed decisions:

1. Diversify Your Sources: Relying solely on mainstream media outlets can limit your exposure to different perspectives. Seek out alternative news sources, independent journalists, and fact-checking organizations to gain a more comprehensive understanding of current events.
2. Fact-Check and Verify: Before accepting information as truth, take the time to fact-check and verify the claims being made. Look for multiple sources and cross-reference information to ensure its accuracy.
3. Develop Critical Thinking Skills: Question the motives behind the information being presented. Consider the potential biases of the sources and critically analyze the evidence provided. Look for logical fallacies and inconsistencies in the arguments being made.
4. Stay Informed and Engaged: Actively seek out information and stay informed about current events. Engage in discussions with others, share different perspectives, and encourage open dialogue. By staying engaged, you can challenge the deep state's narrative and contribute to a more informed society.
5. Support Independent Media: Independent media outlets often provide alternative viewpoints and investigative journalism that challenges the mainstream narrative. Support these outlets by subscribing, sharing their content, and contributing to their work.
6. Practice Media Literacy: Educate yourself and others about media literacy. Teach critical thinking skills to younger generations and encourage them to question the information they encounter. By promoting media literacy, we can empower individuals to think critically and resist manipulation.

Breaking free from media influence is a crucial step in unveiling the deep state's agenda and reclaiming our freedom. By recognizing propaganda techniques, diversifying our sources, and developing critical thinking skills, we can become active participants in shaping our own narrative and creating a brighter future based on truth and justice.

The Deep State's Influence on Politics

7.1 Corruption and the Deep State

Corruption is a cancer that eats away at the very fabric of society. It undermines trust, erodes democratic values, and perpetuates inequality. Unfortunately, corruption is not limited to individual actors or isolated incidents. It can also be systemic, deeply ingrained within the structures of power. This is where the concept of the deep state comes into play.

The deep state refers to a shadowy network of individuals and institutions that operate behind the scenes, exerting influence and control over political, economic, and social affairs. It is characterized by secrecy, manipulation, and a disregard for the rule of law. In the context of corruption, the deep state plays a significant role in perpetuating and protecting corrupt practices.

One of the ways in which the deep state engages in corruption is through the manipulation of political processes. Political parties, which are meant to represent the interests of the people, can become vehicles for the deep state's agenda. By infiltrating and influencing these parties, the deep state ensures that its interests are prioritized over those of the general public.

The deep state's grip on political parties is often achieved through a combination of financial influence, blackmail, and coercion. By providing financial support to candidates and parties, the deep state can ensure that its preferred candidates are elected into positions of power. In return, these candidates are expected to further the deep state's agenda and protect its interests.

Furthermore, the deep state relies on the infiltration and manipulation of key institutions within the political system. This includes the judiciary, law enforcement agencies, and regulatory bodies. By placing individuals loyal to the deep state in positions of power within these institutions, the deep state can ensure that its corrupt practices go unchecked and unpunished.

The consequences of corruption within the deep state are far-reaching. It undermines the principles of democracy and the rule of law, as decisions are made based on personal gain rather than the public interest. It also perpetuates inequality, as resources and opportunities are concentrated in the hands of a few, while the majority of the population suffers.

To expose and combat corruption within the deep state, it is crucial to shine a light on its operations and hold those responsible accountable. Whistleblowers play a vital role in this process, as they have the courage to come forward and reveal the truth. However, the consequences of exposing the deep state can be severe, with whistleblowers often facing retaliation and persecution.

Revelations and leaks are another powerful tool in unmasking corruption within the deep state. These leaks can expose the inner workings of the deep state, revealing the extent of its corruption and manipulation. They can also serve as a wake-up call to the general public, prompting them to demand transparency and accountability from their leaders.

However, the fight against corruption within the deep state is not an easy one. The deep state has significant resources and influence at its disposal, making it difficult to dismantle. It requires a collective effort from citizens, civil society organizations, and the media to expose and challenge the deep state's corrupt practices.

In conclusion, corruption and the deep state go hand in hand. The deep state's manipulation of political processes and infiltration of key institutions perpetuate corrupt practices and undermine democratic values. Exposing and combating corruption within the deep state requires the courage of whistleblowers, the power of revelations and leaks, and the collective effort of citizens. Only through continued vigilance and a commitment to transparency and accountability can we hope to root out corruption and build a brighter future for all.

the deep state's grip on political parties is a crucial aspect to understand in order to fully comprehend their agenda and the extent of their influence. Political parties play a significant role in shaping the policies and direction of a nation, and the deep state has strategically infiltrated and manipulated these parties to further their own objectives.

One of the primary ways the deep state exerts its control over political parties is through the selection and funding of candidates. By supporting and promoting candidates who align with their interests, the deep state ensures that their agenda continues to be advanced, regardless of which party is in power. This control extends beyond just the presidential race, but also encompasses congressional, gubernatorial, and local elections.

The deep state's grip on political parties is further strengthened through the use of lobbying and campaign contributions. Powerful interest groups and corporations, which are often closely tied to the deep state, provide substantial financial support to candidates who are willing to promote their agenda. This financial dependency creates a system where politicians are beholden to the deep state's interests, rather than the needs and desires of the people they are meant to represent.

In addition to financial control, the deep state also utilizes a network of influential individuals within political parties to ensure their agenda is implemented. These individuals, often referred to as "establishment figures," hold positions of power and influence within the party structure. They work behind the scenes to shape party platforms, control the narrative, and marginalize dissenting voices. By controlling key positions within the party apparatus, the deep state can effectively steer the direction of the party and suppress any opposition to their agenda.

Another tactic employed by the deep state is the manipulation of party platforms and policy positions. They strategically push for policies that align with their objectives, such as increased government surveillance, military interventionism, and the erosion of civil liberties. Through their influence over party leaders and the media, they shape the narrative and public perception, making it difficult for alternative viewpoints to gain traction within the party.

Furthermore, the deep state's grip on political parties extends to the realm of intelligence agencies and national security apparatus. These agencies often operate independently of elected officials and exert significant influence over policy decisions. The deep state utilizes this influence to ensure that their agenda is prioritized and implemented, regardless of the party in power. This creates a situation where elected officials may be unaware of the true extent of the deep state's control and are unable to effectively challenge their authority.

It is important to note that the deep state's influence is not limited to a single political party. They have infiltrated and manipulated both major parties, ensuring that their agenda remains intact regardless of which party is in power. This bipartisan control allows the deep state to maintain their grip on the political landscape and continue advancing their objectives without significant opposition.

To break free from the deep state's grip on political parties, it is crucial for individuals to become aware of their tactics and question the narratives presented by mainstream media and establishment figures. It is essential to support independent candidates who are not beholden to the deep state's interests and to actively engage in grassroots movements that seek to challenge the status quo.

By empowering ourselves with knowledge, actively participating in the political process, and demanding transparency and accountability from our elected officials, we can begin to weaken the deep state's grip on political parties. It is through collective action and a commitment to democratic values that we can restore the power to the people and ensure that our political system truly represents the will of the citizens.

In the next section, we will delve deeper into the methods of infiltration and manipulation employed by the deep state, shedding light on their tactics and strategies to maintain control over the political landscape.

the infiltration and manipulation tactics employed by the deep state. In this section, we will delve into the methods used by the deep state to infiltrate various institutions and manipulate them to serve their agenda.

One of the key strategies employed by the deep state is the infiltration of political parties, government agencies, and other influential organizations. By placing their operatives in key positions, they are able to exert control and influence over decision-making processes. These operatives often work behind the scenes, pulling the strings and ensuring that their agenda is advanced.

The deep state's infiltration efforts extend beyond just political parties. They also target media organizations, think tanks, and academic institutions. By controlling the narrative and shaping public opinion, they are able to manipulate the masses and maintain their grip on power. Through strategic placement of their agents, they can ensure that their agenda is promoted and dissenting voices are silenced.

One of the most effective ways the deep state infiltrates institutions is through the use of blackmail and coercion. They gather compromising information on individuals in positions of power and use it as leverage to ensure their compliance. This allows them to control key decision-makers and ensure that their agenda is followed.

Another tactic employed by the deep state is the manipulation of public opinion through propaganda and disinformation campaigns. By controlling the flow of information, they are able to shape public perception and control the narrative. Through the use of media outlets and social media platforms, they disseminate their propaganda and suppress dissenting voices. This manipulation of information allows them to maintain their control and prevent the truth from being exposed.

In addition to infiltration and manipulation, the deep state also utilizes divide and conquer tactics to maintain their power. By creating divisions among the population based on race, religion, or political affiliation, they are able to divert attention away from their true agenda. This strategy allows them to keep the masses distracted and prevents them from uniting against their common oppressor.

The deep state's manipulation extends beyond just institutions and public opinion. They also manipulate the economy to serve their interests. Through their control of financial institutions and regulatory bodies, they are able to manipulate markets and ensure that wealth is concentrated in the hands of a few. This economic manipulation allows them to maintain their power and control over the middle class, who are often the hardest hit by their policies.

It is important to recognize the tactics employed by the deep state and remain vigilant against their infiltration and manipulation. By staying informed and questioning the narratives presented to us, we can begin to break free from their control. Building a resistance movement and working towards protecting our rights and liberties is crucial in countering their influence.

In conclusion, the deep state's infiltration and manipulation tactics are pervasive and far-reaching. By infiltrating institutions, manipulating public opinion, and controlling the economy, they are able to maintain their power and advance their agenda. It is up to us, the people, to recognize these tactics and work towards exposing the truth. Only through awareness, resistance, and a united front can we hope to overcome the deep state's influence and restore true democracy.

the deep state's agenda to control and manipulate the population. In this section, we will delve into the dark and sinister world of the puppet masters behind the scenes, who pull the strings of power and influence in our political system.

The term "puppet masters" refers to the individuals or groups who exert control over politicians and government officials, shaping their decisions and actions to align with their own hidden agendas. These puppet masters operate in the shadows, hidden from public view, but their influence is far-reaching and pervasive.

One of the key tactics employed by the puppet masters is the infiltration and manipulation of political parties. They strategically place their own people within the ranks of these parties, ensuring that their interests are protected and advanced. By controlling both major political parties, they effectively limit the choices available to the public, creating an illusion of democracy while maintaining their grip on power.

The puppet masters also utilize corruption as a means to control politicians. Through bribery, blackmail, and other illicit means, they ensure that those in positions of power remain loyal to their cause. This corruption extends beyond individual politicians and seeps into the very fabric of our political system, eroding the trust and faith that the public has in their elected representatives.

Furthermore, the puppet masters exert their influence through the manipulation of media and propaganda. They control the flow of information, shaping public opinion and controlling the narrative to suit their own interests. By controlling the media, they can sway public opinion, suppress dissenting voices, and maintain their hold on power.

It is important to recognize that the puppet masters are not limited to any particular political party or ideology. They operate across party lines, using their influence to further their own agenda, regardless of the consequences for the people they are supposed to serve. Their allegiance lies not with the citizens, but with their own self-interest and the consolidation of power.

Exposing the puppet masters requires a concerted effort from the public. It requires a willingness to question the status quo, to challenge the narratives presented to us, and to seek out the truth for ourselves. It requires us to be vigilant and discerning consumers of information, not easily swayed by propaganda or manipulated by those in power.

Whistleblowers play a crucial role in exposing the puppet masters. These brave individuals risk their careers, their reputations, and even their lives to bring to light the hidden truths and corruption that permeate our political system. Their revelations and leaks provide valuable insights into the inner workings of the deep state and the puppet masters who control it.

However, the fight against the puppet masters is not without consequences. Those who dare to expose the truth often face retaliation and persecution. They may be labeled as conspiracy theorists, dismissed as troublemakers, or even targeted for harm. The deep state will stop at nothing to protect its secrets and maintain its grip on power.

But despite the risks, the fight for truth and justice must continue. We must come together as a society, united in our pursuit of transparency, accountability, and a government that truly serves the people. We must demand an end to the puppet masters' control and work towards a system that is truly representative of the will and interests of the citizens.

In conclusion, the puppet masters behind the deep state's agenda wield immense power and influence over our political system. They infiltrate political parties, manipulate media, and use corruption as a tool to control politicians. Exposing these puppet masters requires a vigilant and discerning public, supported by brave whistleblowers who are willing to risk everything for the truth. The fight against the puppet masters is not without consequences, but it is a fight that must be waged for the sake of our democracy and the future of our nation.

The Deep State's Economic Agenda

the deep state's agenda of controlling the global economy. This chapter will delve into the strategies and tactics employed by the deep state to manipulate and dominate the economic landscape on a global scale.

The deep state's control over the global economy is a crucial aspect of their overall agenda. By exerting influence over financial systems, trade policies, and international organizations, they are able to shape the economic landscape to their advantage. This control allows them to consolidate power, amass wealth, and further their own interests at the expense of the general population.

One of the primary methods employed by the deep state to control the global economy is through financial manipulation. They utilize their influence over central banks, multinational corporations, and financial institutions to manipulate markets, currencies, and interest rates. By artificially inflating or deflating the value of currencies, they can create economic instability and exploit the resulting chaos for their own gain.

Furthermore, the deep state's financial manipulation extends to the stock market and other investment vehicles. Through insider trading, market manipulation, and the dissemination of false information, they are able to control stock prices and profit from the resulting fluctuations. This not only allows them to accumulate vast amounts of wealth but also gives them the power to influence corporate decision-making and shape the direction of industries.

The impact of the deep state's economic agenda is particularly felt by the middle class. As wealth becomes increasingly concentrated in the hands of a few, income inequality rises, and the middle class is squeezed. The deep state's policies and practices favor the elite, while the middle class struggles to make ends meet. This deliberate erosion of the middle class serves to further consolidate power and control within the hands of the deep state.

While the deep state benefits from their economic control, it is important to recognize that they are not the ultimate beneficiaries. Behind the scenes, there are shadowy figures and entities who reap the rewards of the deep state's economic agenda. These individuals and organizations operate in the shadows, profiting from the chaos and instability created by the deep state's manipulation. By obscuring their true identities and motives, they are able to continue their exploitation unchecked.

The deep state's control over the global economy extends beyond national borders. They utilize international organizations such as the International Monetary Fund (IMF), World Bank, and World Trade Organization (WTO) to further their economic agenda. Through these organizations, they impose policies and regulations that benefit their interests while disregarding the needs and aspirations of sovereign nations.

Additionally, the deep state's economic agenda is intertwined with global conflicts. By fueling and perpetuating conflicts around the world, they create opportunities for economic exploitation and resource extraction. Through their control over military-industrial complexes and arms sales, they profit from the suffering and destruction caused by these conflicts.

The deep state's quest for global domination is driven by their insatiable thirst for power and control. By manipulating the global economy, they are able to exert influence over nations, governments, and individuals. This control allows them to shape policies, dictate terms, and maintain their grip on power.

However, it is important to note that the deep state's control over the global economy is not absolute. There are individuals and groups who resist their influence and work towards creating alternative economic systems that prioritize fairness, equality, and sustainability. By supporting local economies, promoting ethical business practices, and advocating for transparency, these individuals and groups challenge the deep state's dominance and offer hope for a brighter future.

In conclusion, the deep state's control over the global economy is a central component of their agenda. Through financial manipulation, exploitation of the middle class, and influence over international organizations, they consolidate power and further their own interests. However, there are those who resist their influence and work towards creating a more equitable and just economic system. It is through continued vigilance, empowerment of the people, and collective action that we can challenge the deep state's control and strive for a future that prioritizes the well-being of all.

the deep state's financial manipulation. This chapter will delve into the intricate web of economic control that the deep state has woven, and how it affects the middle class and the true beneficiaries of their actions.

The deep state's financial manipulation is a crucial aspect of their overall agenda. By exerting control over the global economy, they are able to shape the world according to their desires and maintain their grip on power. Through various means, they manipulate markets, currencies, and institutions to serve their own interests, often at the expense of the middle class and the general population.

One of the primary tools the deep state employs in their financial manipulation is the control of central banks. These institutions, such as the Federal Reserve in the United States, have the power to influence interest rates, regulate the money supply, and shape monetary policy. By controlling these levers of economic power, the deep state can effectively steer the direction of the economy and benefit their chosen beneficiaries.

Through their control of central banks, the deep state can create artificial booms and busts in the economy. They manipulate interest rates to encourage borrowing and spending during times of economic expansion, leading to unsustainable levels of debt. This debt burden falls disproportionately on the middle class, who are often left struggling to make ends meet while the true beneficiaries of the deep state's actions continue to amass wealth.

Furthermore, the deep state's financial manipulation extends beyond the domestic economy. They exert influence over international financial institutions such as the International Monetary Fund (IMF) and the World Bank, using these organizations to further their agenda on a global scale. By controlling these institutions, they can dictate economic policies to countries around the world, ensuring that their interests are protected and advanced.

The deep state's financial manipulation also involves the manipulation of markets. Through their vast network of connections and insider knowledge, they are able to exploit market inefficiencies and rig the game in their favor. This includes activities such as insider trading, market manipulation, and the use of high-frequency trading algorithms to gain an unfair advantage. These practices not only undermine the integrity of financial markets but also contribute to the growing wealth inequality that plagues societies worldwide.

The middle class bears the brunt of the deep state's financial manipulation. As the backbone of the economy, they are often the ones who suffer the most during economic downturns and financial crises. While the deep state's chosen beneficiaries are shielded from the consequences of their actions, the middle class is left to bear the burden of job losses, foreclosures, and financial insecurity.

The deep state's financial manipulation also has far-reaching implications for democracy and the functioning of governments. By exerting control over the economy, they can influence political decisions and shape policies that serve their interests. This undermines the democratic process and erodes trust in government institutions, as the true power lies in the hands of unelected individuals who operate behind the scenes.

To combat the deep state's financial manipulation, it is crucial for the middle class and the general population to become aware of their actions and their impact on society. By educating themselves about the inner workings of the economy and the tactics employed by the deep state, individuals can better understand how their financial well-being is being manipulated.

Additionally, it is essential to support policies and initiatives that promote transparency, accountability, and fairness in the financial system. This includes advocating for stricter regulations on financial institutions, promoting ethical business practices, and demanding greater oversight of central banks and international financial institutions.

Ultimately, the battle against the deep state's financial manipulation is a fight for economic justice and equality. By exposing their actions and working towards a more equitable and transparent financial system, we can begin to dismantle the deep state's grip on power and create a future where the middle class and the general population can thrive.

the deep state's economic agenda. In this section, we will explore the impact of the deep state's economic policies on the middle class.

The middle class has long been considered the backbone of any thriving economy. It is the segment of society that drives consumer spending, invests in education and healthcare, and fuels innovation and entrepreneurship. However, the deep state's economic agenda has had a detrimental effect on the middle class, leading to a widening wealth gap and a decline in economic mobility.

One of the key ways the deep state has impacted the middle class is through its control of the global economy. By manipulating financial markets, influencing trade policies, and promoting multinational corporations, the deep state has created an environment that favors the wealthy elite at the expense of the middle class. This has resulted in job losses, stagnant wages, and a decrease in job security for many middle-class workers.

Furthermore, the deep state's financial manipulation has led to economic crises and recessions that disproportionately affect the middle class. Through their control of central banks and financial institutions, the deep state has the power to artificially inflate or deflate asset prices, manipulate interest rates, and create speculative bubbles. These actions often result in the loss of savings, investments, and retirement funds for middle-class individuals and families.

Another aspect of the deep state's economic agenda that impacts the middle class is the erosion of worker rights and protections. Through their influence on labor laws and regulations, the deep state has weakened unions, undermined collective bargaining, and promoted policies that prioritize corporate interests over the well-being of workers. This has led to a decline in job security, reduced benefits, and an increase in precarious employment for many middle-class workers.

Additionally, the deep state's economic policies have contributed to the rising cost of living for the middle class. As the wealthy elite accumulate more wealth and power, they are able to influence policies that favor their interests, such as tax cuts for the rich and corporations. This often results in a heavier tax burden for the middle class, who are left to bear the brunt of funding public services and infrastructure.

Moreover, the deep state's economic agenda has also impacted the middle class through its control of the financial sector. By promoting policies that prioritize the interests of big banks and Wall Street, the deep state has created an environment that allows for risky financial practices and predatory lending. This has led to the housing crisis, where many middle-class families lost their homes due to subprime mortgages and foreclosure.

The deep state's economic agenda has also hindered upward mobility for the middle class. As wealth becomes concentrated in the hands of a few, opportunities for social and economic advancement become limited. The middle class, once seen as a pathway to prosperity, is now facing barriers to upward mobility, such as rising education costs, limited access to affordable healthcare, and a lack of investment in infrastructure and public services.

In conclusion, the deep state's economic agenda has had a profound impact on the middle class. Through their control of the global economy, financial manipulation, erosion of worker rights, rising cost of living, and hindrance of upward mobility, the deep state has created an environment that favors the wealthy elite at the expense of the middle class. It is crucial for the middle class to recognize these impacts and work towards reclaiming their economic power and influence. Only through collective action and a commitment to economic justice can the middle class hope to regain its rightful place as the driving force behind a prosperous and equitable society.

the deep state's economic agenda. In this section, we will delve into the true beneficiaries of the deep state's economic manipulation and control. It is important to understand that the deep state operates behind the scenes, pulling the strings of power and influence to serve their own interests, often at the expense of the middle class and the general population.

One of the primary objectives of the deep state's economic agenda is to maintain control over the global economy. Through their influence in international organizations and financial institutions, they ensure that policies and regulations are implemented to benefit their own interests. This control allows them to manipulate markets, currencies, and trade agreements to their advantage, while ordinary citizens bear the brunt of economic instability and inequality.

The deep state's financial manipulation is a key tool in their economic agenda. They have the power to create and control money through central banks and financial institutions. By manipulating interest rates, printing money, and engaging in speculative activities, they can artificially inflate or deflate economies, causing booms and busts that further consolidate their power and wealth. This manipulation allows them to profit from the suffering of others, as they can buy up assets at rock-bottom prices during economic crises.

The impact of the deep state's economic agenda is particularly felt by the middle class. As the backbone of society, the middle class is essential for a thriving economy and a stable society. However, the deep state's policies often lead to the erosion of the middle class, as wealth becomes concentrated in the hands of a few. Through outsourcing, automation, and unfair trade practices, they undermine job security and wage growth, leaving many struggling to make ends meet.

While the middle class suffers, the true beneficiaries of the deep state's economic agenda are the wealthy elite and multinational corporations. These powerful entities have the resources and connections to navigate the complex web of regulations and loopholes created by the deep state. They can exploit tax havens, engage in offshore banking, and receive bailouts and subsidies, all while avoiding their fair share of taxes and responsibilities.

The deep state's economic agenda also extends beyond national borders. Through their influence in international organizations such as the World Bank, International Monetary Fund, and World Trade Organization, they shape global economic policies to their advantage. This allows them to exploit developing countries, extract resources, and maintain a stranglehold on the global economy. By controlling the flow of capital and resources, they ensure that their interests are protected, regardless of the consequences for ordinary people around the world.

It is crucial to recognize that the deep state's economic agenda is not driven by a desire for the common good or the well-being of the majority. Instead, it is motivated by a relentless pursuit of power, control, and wealth. By maintaining their grip on the global economy, they can perpetuate their influence and ensure their continued dominance over political systems, media, and society as a whole.

However, unveiling the true beneficiaries of the deep state's economic agenda is a step towards reclaiming our power and creating a more just and equitable society. By exposing their tactics and raising awareness, we can challenge their control and demand accountability. It is up to us, the people, to come together, resist their influence, and work towards a brighter future where economic power is distributed more fairly and the well-being of all is prioritized over the interests of a few.

The Deep State's Global Reach

the deep state's agenda of global domination and control. In this section, we will explore the deep state's influence beyond borders and how it extends its reach through international organizations and its role in global conflicts.

The deep state's power and influence are not confined to the borders of a single nation. It operates on a global scale, utilizing various means to further its agenda and maintain control over nations and their populations. One of the key ways it achieves this is through its involvement in international organizations.

International organizations such as the United Nations, World Bank, International Monetary Fund, and World Trade Organization play a significant role in shaping global policies and agendas. These organizations are often influenced by the deep state, with key individuals strategically placed to ensure the deep state's interests are served.

Through these organizations, the deep state can exert its influence over various aspects of global governance, including economic policies, trade agreements, and even military interventions. By manipulating these organizations, the deep state can shape the world according to its own agenda, often at the expense of national sovereignty and the well-being of ordinary citizens.

Furthermore, the deep state's influence extends to global conflicts. It has been known to exploit and manipulate conflicts for its own gain, often fueling tensions and perpetuating violence to further its objectives. By instigating or prolonging conflicts, the deep state can create a state of chaos and instability, which it then uses as a pretext to intervene and exert control.

In many instances, the deep state has been involved in covert operations, arming and supporting various factions to serve its interests. These actions not only perpetuate conflicts but also contribute to the suffering of innocent civilians caught in the crossfire. The deep state's role in global conflicts is often hidden from public view, with the media and propaganda machinery working to shape public perception and maintain the illusion of noble intentions.

The deep state's quest for global domination is driven by a desire for power, control, and the consolidation of wealth. It seeks to establish a world order in which it holds the reins of power, dictating policies and decisions that benefit its own interests. This global agenda is often masked under the guise of promoting democracy, human rights, and stability, but in reality, it serves to further entrench the deep state's control and suppress dissent.

The deep state's influence beyond borders is not limited to overt actions. It also operates through covert means, such as economic manipulation, espionage, and cyber warfare. By infiltrating foreign governments, financial institutions, and technology networks, the deep state can gather intelligence, exert control, and manipulate events to its advantage.

The consequences of the deep state's influence beyond borders are far-reaching. It undermines the sovereignty of nations, erodes democratic values, and perpetuates inequality and injustice. Ordinary citizens around the world bear the brunt of these actions, as their rights and freedoms are curtailed, and their voices are silenced.

However, there is hope for a brighter future. Awareness and resistance are key to countering the deep state's influence. By recognizing the signs of the deep state's presence and understanding its tactics, individuals and communities can work together to expose its agenda and protect their rights and liberties.

It is crucial for people to engage in civic participation, hold their governments accountable, and demand transparency and accountability. By standing up against the deep state's influence, individuals can contribute to the restoration of trust in government and the preservation of democratic values.

In conclusion, the deep state's influence extends beyond national borders, infiltrating international organizations and manipulating global conflicts. Its agenda of global domination and control threatens the sovereignty of nations and the well-being of ordinary citizens. However, through awareness, resistance, and collective action, there is hope for a future free from the deep state's grip. It is up to individuals to empower themselves and work towards a world that values freedom, justice, and democracy.

the deep state's global reach and influence through international organizations.

9.2 International Organizations and the Deep State

The deep state's agenda extends far beyond the borders of any single nation. It operates on a global scale, utilizing international organizations to further its objectives and maintain control over the world's affairs. These organizations, often seen as symbols of unity and cooperation, are in reality tools of the deep state, serving its interests and perpetuating its power.

One such organization is the United Nations (UN), which was established in 1945 with the aim of promoting peace, security, and cooperation among nations. While the UN's stated goals may seem noble, it has become increasingly clear that it has been infiltrated and manipulated by the deep state. The deep state uses the UN as a platform to advance its own agenda, exerting influence over member states and shaping global policies to align with its objectives.

Through the UN, the deep state seeks to consolidate power and control over nations by promoting global governance and eroding national sovereignty. It does this by advocating for international treaties and agreements that undermine the rights and freedoms of individuals and nations. These treaties often serve as a pretext for the deep state to exert control over various aspects of society, including the economy, the environment, and even individual behavior.

Another international organization that plays a significant role in the deep state's global reach is the World Health Organization (WHO). While the WHO is ostensibly tasked with safeguarding global health, it has been co-opted by the deep state to further its own interests. The deep state uses the WHO to manipulate public health crises and shape public opinion, often to the detriment of individual freedoms and national sovereignty.

One example of the deep state's influence through the WHO is its response to the COVID-19 pandemic. The deep state, through its control of the organization, has used the pandemic as an opportunity to exert control over nations, implement draconian measures, and consolidate its power. By promoting fear and uncertainty, the deep state has been able to manipulate public opinion and push for policies that further its agenda, such as mandatory vaccinations and increased surveillance.

The deep state's influence is not limited to these two organizations alone. It extends to a wide range of international bodies, including the International Monetary Fund (IMF), the World Bank, and the World Trade Organization (WTO). These organizations, which are meant to promote economic stability and global trade, have been co-opted by the deep state to serve its own interests.

Through the IMF and the World Bank, the deep state exerts control over the global economy, manipulating currencies, imposing austerity measures, and perpetuating a system of debt slavery. By controlling the flow of capital and dictating economic policies, the deep state ensures that its interests are protected and its power is maintained.

The WTO, on the other hand, serves as a mechanism for the deep state to shape global trade policies in its favor. By promoting free trade agreements that benefit multinational corporations and undermine local industries, the deep state consolidates its economic power and ensures the dominance of its preferred players.

It is important to recognize the deep state's influence through these international organizations and to understand that their actions are not always in the best interest of the people they claim to serve. The deep state operates behind the scenes, manipulating policies and shaping global events to further its own agenda. By understanding the true nature of these organizations and their relationship with the deep state, we can begin to break free from their influence and work towards a brighter future based on freedom, democracy, and individual sovereignty.

the deep state's global agenda. In this section, we will explore the role of the deep state in global conflicts and how it manipulates these conflicts to further its own objectives.

The deep state's influence extends far beyond national borders. It operates on a global scale, using various tactics to exploit and control conflicts around the world. By understanding its role in global conflicts, we can gain insight into its motives and strategies.

One of the key ways the deep state exerts its influence is by fueling and perpetuating conflicts in different regions. It does this by supporting and arming various factions, often playing both sides of the conflict to maintain a balance of power that serves its interests. By keeping conflicts alive, the deep state can ensure a constant state of chaos and instability, which allows it to exert control and manipulate events to its advantage.

The deep state's involvement in global conflicts is not limited to direct military intervention. It also uses economic and political means to shape the outcomes of these conflicts. Through its control of international organizations and financial institutions, the deep state can impose sanctions, manipulate currencies, and control the flow of aid and resources to influence the course of conflicts.

One example of the deep state's role in global conflicts is its involvement in the Middle East. The region has been plagued by conflicts for decades, and the deep state has played a significant role in perpetuating and escalating these conflicts. By supporting and arming different factions, the deep state has been able to maintain a state of instability, ensuring its continued influence and control over the region's resources.

Another example is the deep state's involvement in Africa. The continent has been a battleground for various conflicts, often fueled by external powers seeking to exploit its rich natural resources. The deep state has been known to support and arm rebel groups, dictators, and warlords, all in the pursuit of its own economic and geopolitical interests.

In addition to fueling conflicts, the deep state also uses these conflicts as a pretext for military interventions. By creating or exacerbating crises, it can justify military actions under the guise of humanitarian intervention or national security. These interventions often serve to further the deep state's agenda, whether it be securing strategic resources, expanding its military presence, or establishing control over key regions.

It is important to note that the deep state's involvement in global conflicts is not driven by a desire for peace or stability. On the contrary, it thrives in a state of chaos and conflict, as it allows for greater control and manipulation. By perpetuating conflicts and exploiting the resulting instability, the deep state can advance its own interests and maintain its grip on power.

Understanding the deep state's role in global conflicts is crucial for those seeking to challenge its influence and work towards a more peaceful and just world. By exposing its tactics and motives, we can begin to dismantle the structures that enable its power and create space for genuine dialogue, cooperation, and conflict resolution.

In the next section, we will delve into the deep state's quest for global domination and the strategies it employs to achieve this goal. We will explore its influence over international organizations, its economic agenda, and the methods it uses to control and manipulate governments worldwide. By shedding light on these aspects, we can better understand the true nature of the deep state and work towards a future free from its grip.

the deep state's quest for global domination. This chapter delves into the extent of the deep state's influence beyond national borders and its involvement in international organizations and global conflicts. It uncovers the strategies employed by the deep state to expand its power and control on a global scale.

The Deep State's Global Reach

The deep state's influence extends far beyond the borders of any single nation. It operates on a global scale, leveraging its power and resources to shape the course of international affairs. Through its network of operatives and alliances, the deep state seeks to control key institutions and manipulate global events to further its own agenda.

International Organizations and the Deep State

One of the primary avenues through which the deep state exerts its influence globally is by infiltrating and manipulating international organizations. These organizations, such as the United Nations, World Bank, and International Monetary Fund, are intended to promote cooperation and address global challenges. However, the deep state sees them as tools to advance its own interests.

By placing its operatives in key positions within these organizations, the deep state can shape policies, control funding, and influence decision-making processes. This allows them to steer the direction of global initiatives, such as sustainable development goals, climate change agreements, and humanitarian interventions, to align with their own objectives.

Global Conflicts and the Deep State's Role

The deep state also plays a significant role in fueling and perpetuating global conflicts. By manipulating geopolitical tensions and supporting proxy wars, the deep state can create chaos and instability, which it then exploits to further its own agenda. This can involve arming and funding rebel groups, supporting regime change operations, or even orchestrating false flag attacks to justify military interventions.

Through these actions, the deep state not only maintains a state of perpetual conflict but also profits from the sale of weapons and the control of strategic resources. By perpetuating global conflicts, the deep state can exert control over nations and shape the geopolitical landscape to its advantage.

The Quest for Global Domination

At the heart of the deep state's global reach lies its quest for global domination. The deep state seeks to establish a world order in which it holds unrivaled power and control over all aspects of society. This includes political systems, economic structures, and even individual freedoms.

To achieve this, the deep state employs a multi-faceted approach. It uses its influence in international organizations to shape global policies and agendas. It manipulates global conflicts to create chaos and instability, allowing it to exert control over nations. It also leverages its economic power to manipulate markets and control resources.

By consolidating its power on a global scale, the deep state aims to create a system in which it can dictate the course of human history. This quest for global domination is driven by a desire for control, wealth, and the preservation of its own interests.

The Resistance and the Fight for a Better Future

Despite the deep state's formidable reach and influence, there is hope for a brighter future. The resistance against the deep state's agenda is growing, fueled by a desire for truth, justice, and the preservation of democratic values.

People around the world are becoming increasingly aware of the deep state's machinations and are actively working to expose its actions. Whistleblowers and courageous individuals are stepping forward to reveal the truth, risking their lives and livelihoods to fight against the deep state's global domination.

The fight for a better future requires continued vigilance, empowerment of the people, and a call to action. It is through awareness, education, and collective action that we can challenge the deep state's influence and work towards a world that values freedom, democracy, and justice for all.

In the face of the deep state's quest for global domination, it is crucial to remain steadfast in our commitment to truth, justice, and the preservation of democratic values. Together, we can build a future where the power of the deep state is dismantled, and the voices of the people are heard and respected.

Unmasking the Deep State

the unmasking of the deep state by courageous whistleblowers. These individuals, driven by a sense of duty and a commitment to truth, have risked their careers, reputations, and even their lives to expose the hidden agenda of the deep state.

Whistleblowers play a crucial role in unveiling the truth and shedding light on the dark corners of power. They are individuals who have insider knowledge of the deep state's operations and are willing to come forward and expose the corruption, manipulation, and abuse of power that exists within the system.

These brave individuals often face significant personal and professional consequences for their actions. They may be subjected to harassment, intimidation, and even legal repercussions. Despite these risks, whistleblowers are driven by a deep sense of justice and a belief in the importance of holding those in power accountable.

One notable example of a whistleblower is Edward Snowden, a former National Security Agency (NSA) contractor who exposed the mass surveillance programs conducted by the US government. Snowden's revelations shocked the world and sparked a global debate on privacy, surveillance, and government overreach. His actions exposed the deep state's disregard for individual rights and liberties, and the extent to which they were willing to go to maintain control and power.

Another courageous whistleblower is Chelsea Manning, a former US Army intelligence analyst who leaked classified documents to WikiLeaks. Manning's leaks exposed war crimes committed by the US military in Iraq and Afghanistan, including the killing of innocent civilians. Her actions shed light on the deep state's involvement in illegal and unethical activities, and the lengths they would go to protect their interests.

These whistleblowers, along with many others, have faced severe consequences for their actions. Snowden was forced to seek asylum in Russia to avoid prosecution, while Manning was imprisoned for several years before her sentence was commuted. Their sacrifices serve as a reminder of the immense courage it takes to expose the deep state's secrets.

Whistleblowers are not only individuals within government agencies or intelligence organizations. They can also be journalists, activists, or concerned citizens who stumble upon information that reveals the true nature of the deep state's agenda. These individuals often face significant challenges in bringing their revelations to light, as they may encounter resistance from powerful institutions and face attempts to discredit or silence them.

The importance of whistleblowers cannot be overstated. Their actions have the potential to disrupt the deep state's plans, expose their hidden agenda, and ultimately empower the people to reclaim their rights and liberties. Whistleblowers provide a vital service to society by shining a light on the dark underbelly of power and revealing the truth that has been hidden from the public.

However, it is essential to recognize that whistleblowers often face significant personal and professional challenges. They may be ostracized, vilified, or even targeted for retribution by the deep state and its allies. It is crucial for society to support and protect these individuals, ensuring that they are not silenced or punished for their courageous acts.

In conclusion, whistleblowers are the unsung heroes in the battle against the deep state. Their courage, integrity, and commitment to truth have the power to expose corruption, manipulation, and abuse of power. It is through their actions that we can begin to dismantle the deep state's agenda and work towards a brighter future based on transparency, accountability, and justice. We owe a debt of gratitude to these brave individuals who risk everything to unmask the deep state and protect our freedoms.

the revelations and leaks from brave whistleblowers who have risked their lives to expose the hidden agenda of the deep state.

Throughout history, whistleblowers have played a crucial role in uncovering the truth and shedding light on the dark secrets of those in power. These courageous individuals have risked their careers, reputations, and even their lives to bring to the forefront the hidden agendas and nefarious activities of the deep state.

Revelations and leaks have been instrumental in exposing the deep state's plans for implementing martial law and the use of FEMA camps. These whistleblowers have provided evidence of the deep state's intention to categorize and target specific groups of people through the color system. This system, often disguised as a means of identification or organization, is actually a tool for control and elimination.

The leaks have revealed the grim reality of the deep state's use of guillotines. While historically associated with the French Revolution, these whistleblowers have exposed the implementation of guillotines in modern times. The deep state's agenda includes the loading of bodies into coffin liners and burying them in crypt fields, hidden from public view. These revelations have shocked and horrified many, as they expose the true extent of the deep state's disregard for human life.

The information provided by these brave whistleblowers has also shed light on the motives and objectives of the deep state. Through their leaks, we have come to understand that the deep state's ultimate goal is to control the population and maintain their grip on power. Martial law serves as a means to achieve this objective, allowing the deep state to exert control over every aspect of society.

The revelations and leaks have also exposed the true power players behind the scenes. These individuals, often hidden from public view, manipulate and control governments, economies, and global conflicts to further their own agenda. The deep state's influence extends beyond borders, infiltrating international organizations and perpetuating global conflicts to serve their quest for global domination.

However, the consequences of exposing the deep state are severe. Whistleblowers who come forward to reveal the truth face immense backlash and retaliation. They are often subjected to character assassination, threats, and even physical harm. The deep state will stop at nothing to protect their secrets and maintain their control over the masses.

Despite the risks, these brave individuals continue to fight for truth and justice. Their leaks and revelations have sparked a movement of resistance and awareness. People are waking up to the reality of the deep state's influence and are joining forces to protect their rights and liberties.

The fight against the deep state requires a united front. It demands the courage to recognize the signs of their manipulation and propaganda, and the determination to break free from media influence. It necessitates building a resistance movement that is rooted in awareness and knowledge, and that actively works towards preserving democratic values.

The revelations and leaks have also highlighted the importance of civic engagement. It is through active participation in the political process that we can overcome the deep state's influence. By holding our elected officials accountable and demanding transparency, we can restore trust in government and ensure that the voices of the people are heard.

In conclusion, the revelations and leaks from whistleblowers have been instrumental in unmasking the deep state's agenda. These brave individuals have risked everything to expose the truth and shed light on the hidden activities of those in power. Their leaks have revealed the deep state's plans for martial law, the use of FEMA camps, and the implementation of guillotines. While the consequences of exposing the deep state are severe, the fight for truth and justice continues. It is through resistance, awareness, and civic engagement that we can overcome the deep state's influence and work towards a brighter future.

the exposure of the deep state's agenda can have severe consequences for those who dare to bring it to light. In this section, we will delve into the potential repercussions faced by individuals who expose the deep state and its secretive operations.

1. **Character Assassination**: One of the first consequences faced by whistleblowers and truth-seekers is character assassination. The deep state, with its vast resources and influence, will go to great lengths to discredit and tarnish the reputation of anyone who threatens to expose their hidden agenda. They may employ tactics such as spreading false rumors, manipulating public opinion, and launching smear campaigns to undermine the credibility of those who speak out.

2. **Legal Retaliation**: Exposing the deep state often comes with legal consequences. Whistleblowers may face lawsuits, criminal charges, or even imprisonment. The deep state has the power to manipulate the legal system and use it as a tool to silence dissent and protect their interests. They may exploit loopholes, employ legal technicalities, or even fabricate evidence to ensure that those who challenge their authority face severe legal repercussions.

3. **Loss of Employment and Livelihood**: Individuals who expose the deep state's agenda may find themselves facing professional repercussions. Whistleblowers often face termination from their jobs, making it difficult for them to find employment elsewhere. The deep state can use its influence to blacklist individuals, making it challenging for them to rebuild their careers and support themselves and their families.

4. **Social Isolation and Stigmatization**: Exposing the deep state can lead to social isolation and stigmatization. Whistleblowers may find themselves ostracized by friends, family, and even their communities. The deep state's propaganda machinery can work to portray them as conspiracy theorists, troublemakers, or even threats to national security. This isolation can have a profound impact on the mental and

emotional well-being of those who dare to challenge the deep state's narrative.

1. **Threats and Intimidation**: Whistleblowers and truth-seekers may face threats and intimidation from various sources. The deep state has a network of operatives and assets that can be deployed to harass, intimidate, or even physically harm those who pose a threat to their operations. These threats can range from anonymous phone calls and online harassment to more severe forms of intimidation, including surveillance, break-ins, or even physical violence.

2. **Loss of Privacy and Security**: Exposing the deep state often means sacrificing personal privacy and security. Whistleblowers may find themselves under constant surveillance, both online and offline. Their communications may be monitored, and their personal information may be exposed or leaked. This loss of privacy can have a chilling effect on individuals and deter others from coming forward with valuable information.

3. **Financial Consequences**: Exposing the deep state can also have significant financial consequences. Whistleblowers may face exorbitant legal fees, loss of income, and difficulty finding employment. The deep state can use its influence to freeze assets, seize property, or impose hefty fines on those who threaten their operations. These financial burdens can further hinder the ability of truth-seekers to continue their fight for justice and accountability.

Despite these severe consequences, individuals who expose the deep state's agenda often do so out of a sense of duty, justice, and a desire to protect the rights and freedoms of the people. Their bravery and sacrifice should not be underestimated, as they play a crucial role in uncovering the truth and holding those in power accountable.

It is essential for society to support and protect whistleblowers and truth-seekers, ensuring their safety, providing legal assistance, and offering platforms for their voices to be heard. Only through collective action and a commitment to truth and justice can we hope to overcome the deep state's influence and work towards a brighter future for all.

the fight for truth and justice is a crucial aspect of exposing the deep state's agenda. In this section, we will delve into the various ways individuals and organizations have fought against the deep state's manipulation and worked towards uncovering the truth.

One of the most significant contributors to the fight for truth and justice are whistleblowers. These brave individuals have risked their careers, reputations, and even their lives to expose the hidden workings of the deep state. Whistleblowers play a vital role in shedding light on the dark secrets and corruption that permeate the deep state's operations.

Through their revelations and leaks, whistleblowers have provided invaluable information that has allowed the public to gain a deeper understanding of the deep state's agenda. Their disclosures have exposed the true motives and objectives behind the deep state's actions, revealing the extent of its control and manipulation.

However, the consequences of exposing the deep state can be severe. Whistleblowers often face retaliation, persecution, and even legal consequences for their actions. The deep state will go to great lengths to silence those who threaten to expose its secrets. Despite these risks, whistleblowers continue to come forward, driven by a sense of duty and a commitment to truth and justice.

The fight for truth and justice also involves the tireless efforts of investigative journalists, researchers, and activists. These individuals work diligently to uncover evidence, connect the dots, and expose the deep state's operations. Through their work, they bring attention to the hidden agendas and manipulations that the deep state employs to maintain its power and control.

In recent years, the internet and social media have played a significant role in the fight for truth and justice. Online platforms have provided a space for individuals to share information, discuss theories, and collaborate on uncovering the deep state's agenda. The power of collective knowledge and collaboration has allowed for the dissemination of information that would have otherwise remained hidden.

Citizens have also played a crucial role in the fight for truth and justice. Through grassroots movements and peaceful protests, people have voiced their concerns and demanded transparency and accountability from those in power. The power of the people, when united, can be a formidable force against the deep state's influence.

Legal avenues have also been pursued in the fight for truth and justice. Lawsuits, Freedom of Information Act (FOIA) requests, and other legal mechanisms have been utilized to obtain documents and information that shed light on the deep state's activities. These legal battles are essential in holding the deep state accountable and ensuring that justice is served.

The fight for truth and justice is not without its challenges. The deep state operates in secrecy, employing tactics of misinformation, disinformation, and propaganda to confuse and manipulate the public. It is essential for individuals to be discerning consumers of information, to question narratives, and to seek out multiple sources to form a comprehensive understanding of the truth.

Education and awareness are key in the fight for truth and justice. By educating ourselves and others about the deep state's agenda, we can empower ourselves to recognize its tactics and resist its influence. It is crucial to stay informed, engage in critical thinking, and encourage open dialogue to counter the deep state's attempts to control the narrative.

Ultimately, the fight for truth and justice is a long and arduous battle. It requires unwavering determination, resilience, and a commitment to upholding democratic values and principles. By standing together, supporting whistleblowers, demanding transparency, and holding those in power accountable, we can strive towards a future where truth and justice prevail over the shadows of power.

The Battle for Freedom and Democracy

the battle for freedom and democracy is a crucial aspect of preserving our democratic values. In this section, we will explore the importance of upholding these values and the challenges we face in doing so.

Preserving our democratic values is not just a matter of protecting our individual rights and liberties; it is about safeguarding the very foundation of our society. Democracy is built on the principles of equality, justice, and the rule of law. It is a system that empowers the people to participate in decision-making processes and holds those in power accountable for their actions. However, the deep state's agenda poses a significant threat to these democratic values.

The deep state's objective is to undermine the democratic process and consolidate power in the hands of a few. They seek to manipulate and control the political landscape, the economy, and even the media to further their own interests. By doing so, they erode the trust and faith that citizens have in their government and institutions.

To preserve our democratic values, we must first recognize the importance of civic engagement. Democracy thrives when citizens actively participate in the political process, exercise their right to vote, and hold their elected officials accountable. By staying informed and engaged, we can ensure that our voices are heard and that our interests are represented.

However, the deep state's influence on politics makes it challenging for ordinary citizens to have their voices heard. They infiltrate political parties, manipulate elections, and use their financial power to sway policy decisions. This manipulation undermines the democratic process and creates a system where the interests of the few outweigh the needs of the many.

Overcoming the deep state's influence requires a united effort from the people. We must come together, regardless of our political affiliations, to fight for transparency, accountability, and fairness in our government. By demanding ethical behavior from our elected officials and supporting candidates who prioritize the interests of the people, we can begin to restore trust in our democratic institutions.

Education and awareness are also crucial in preserving our democratic values. We must educate ourselves about the tactics and strategies employed by the deep state to manipulate public opinion and control the narrative. By recognizing propaganda techniques and questioning the information presented to us, we can break free from the influence of media manipulation.

Furthermore, we must foster a culture of critical thinking and open dialogue. Democracy thrives on the exchange of ideas and the ability to have respectful discussions about differing opinions. By promoting a society that values diversity of thought and encourages constructive debate, we can strengthen our democratic values and ensure that all voices are heard.

Restoring trust in government is another essential aspect of preserving our democratic values. The deep state's actions have eroded public trust in our institutions, leading to widespread disillusionment and apathy. To rebuild this trust, we need transparency, accountability, and a commitment to serving the best interests of the people.

Government officials must be held accountable for their actions, and mechanisms for oversight and checks and balances must be strengthened. By promoting transparency in decision-making processes and ensuring that the public has access to accurate and unbiased information, we can begin to restore faith in our democratic institutions.

Preserving our democratic values is not an easy task, but it is a battle worth fighting. It requires the collective effort of engaged citizens, a commitment to education and awareness, and a determination to hold those in power accountable. By preserving our democratic values, we can ensure that our society remains just, equal, and governed by the will of the people.

In the next section, we will explore the importance of civic engagement and how it can empower individuals to make a difference in their communities and in the fight against the deep state's agenda.

the deep state's motives and objectives of controlling the population and maintaining their power. This chapter aims to shed light on the importance of civic engagement in countering the deep state's agenda and restoring trust in government.

Civic engagement is the active participation of individuals in their communities and in the political process. It involves being informed, voicing opinions, and taking action to shape the decisions that affect our lives. In the face of the deep state's influence, civic engagement becomes crucial in safeguarding our freedom and democracy.

One of the primary reasons civic engagement is essential is because it empowers individuals to hold their government accountable. When citizens actively participate in the political process, they become more aware of the actions and policies of those in power. By staying informed and engaged, we can identify when the deep state's agenda is being implemented and take appropriate action to counter it.

Furthermore, civic engagement helps to build a strong and resilient society. When individuals come together to address common issues and work towards shared goals, they create a sense of community and unity. This collective effort can serve as a powerful force against the deep state's divisive tactics and manipulative strategies. By engaging with one another and collaborating on solutions, we can strengthen our democracy and protect our rights and liberties.

Civic engagement also plays a vital role in fostering transparency and accountability within government institutions. When citizens actively participate in public hearings, town hall meetings, and other democratic processes, they can demand transparency from their elected officials. By holding public servants accountable for their actions, we can ensure that the deep state's hidden agenda is exposed and challenged.

Moreover, civic engagement helps to bridge the gap between the government and the people. When individuals actively participate in the political process, they become more informed about the issues that affect their lives. This knowledge allows them to engage in meaningful conversations with their elected representatives, advocating for policies that align with their values and interests. By actively participating in the democratic process, we can ensure that our voices are heard and that our concerns are addressed.

In addition to holding the government accountable, civic engagement also provides an opportunity for individuals to shape the policies and decisions that impact their communities. By actively participating in local government, joining community organizations, and volunteering for causes that matter to us, we can contribute to positive change and make a difference in our society. This active involvement helps to counter the deep state's influence by promoting grassroots movements and initiatives that prioritize the well-being of the people.

Furthermore, civic engagement serves as a powerful tool for education and awareness. By engaging with others and participating in discussions and debates, we can learn from different perspectives and gain a deeper understanding of the issues at hand. This knowledge equips us with the tools to recognize propaganda, misinformation, and manipulation tactics employed by the deep state. By staying informed and educating others, we can collectively resist the deep state's attempts to control the narrative and shape public opinion.

Lastly, civic engagement is essential for restoring trust in government. The deep state's agenda thrives on secrecy, manipulation, and the erosion of public trust. By actively participating in the political process and demanding transparency, we can rebuild trust in our institutions and ensure that they serve the best interests of the people. Through civic engagement, we can create a government that is accountable, responsive, and truly representative of the people it serves.

In conclusion, civic engagement is of utmost importance in countering the deep state's agenda and restoring trust in government. By actively participating in the political process, staying informed, and holding our elected officials accountable, we can safeguard our freedom, protect our democracy, and work towards a brighter future. It is through civic engagement that we can reclaim our power as citizens and ensure that our voices are heard and respected.

the deep state's motives and objectives of controlling the population and maintaining their power. This chapter aims to shed light on the methods and strategies that can be employed to overcome the deep state's influence and restore trust in government.

Understanding the Deep State's Influence

The deep state's influence is pervasive and extends into various aspects of society, including politics, media, and the economy. It operates behind the scenes, manipulating events and shaping public opinion to serve its own interests. Overcoming this influence requires a comprehensive understanding of its tactics and a commitment to preserving democratic values.

Educating and Raising Awareness

One of the most effective ways to overcome the deep state's influence is through education and raising awareness. By providing accurate information and exposing the truth behind their actions, individuals can empower themselves and others to question the narratives presented by the deep state. This can be achieved through independent research, critical thinking, and engaging in open discussions.

Building a Strong Resistance Movement

To counter the deep state's influence, it is crucial to build a strong resistance movement. This movement should be based on the principles of transparency, accountability, and justice. By organizing grassroots efforts, individuals can come together to challenge the deep state's power and demand change. This can involve peaceful protests, advocacy campaigns, and supporting political candidates who prioritize the interests of the people over those of the deep state.

Protecting Rights and Liberties

The deep state's influence often results in the erosion of individual rights and liberties. To overcome this, it is essential to actively protect and defend these rights. This can be achieved through legal means, such as supporting organizations that fight for civil liberties, advocating for constitutional reforms, and holding elected officials accountable for their actions. Additionally, individuals can educate themselves about their rights and actively participate in the democratic process to ensure their voices are heard.

Promoting Transparency and Accountability

Transparency and accountability are crucial in overcoming the deep state's influence. By demanding transparency from government institutions and holding them accountable for their actions, individuals can expose corruption and prevent the deep state from operating in secrecy. This can involve supporting initiatives that promote government transparency, advocating for whistleblower protections, and pushing for independent investigations into deep state activities.

Breaking Free from Media Manipulation

The deep state's control of information through media manipulation is a significant obstacle to overcome. To counter this, individuals must become critical consumers of news and media. By diversifying news sources, fact-checking information, and questioning the narratives presented, individuals can break free from media manipulation and form their own informed opinions. Additionally, supporting independent and alternative media outlets can provide alternative perspectives and challenge the deep state's control over the mainstream media.

Strengthening Democratic Institutions

Overcoming the deep state's influence requires strengthening democratic institutions. This involves promoting transparency, accountability, and integrity within these institutions. By supporting reforms that limit the influence of money in politics, ensuring fair and free elections, and promoting ethical behavior among elected officials, individuals can help restore trust in government and reduce the deep state's hold on power.

Engaging in Civic Participation

Active civic participation is essential in overcoming the deep state's influence. By engaging in the democratic process, individuals can have a direct impact on decision-making and hold elected officials accountable. This can involve voting in elections, attending public meetings, joining community organizations, and participating in grassroots movements. By actively participating in the political process, individuals can help shape policies that reflect the interests of the people rather than the deep state.

Fostering Unity and Collaboration

Overcoming the deep state's influence requires unity and collaboration among individuals who share a common goal. By setting aside differences and focusing on shared values and objectives, individuals can form powerful alliances that can challenge the deep state's power. This can involve reaching out to like-minded individuals, building coalitions, and working together to achieve common objectives. By fostering unity and collaboration, individuals can amplify their voices and increase their impact.

Restoring Trust in Government

Restoring trust in government is crucial in overcoming the deep state's influence. This requires elected officials to prioritize the interests of the people and act with transparency and integrity. Additionally, individuals must actively participate in the democratic process, hold elected officials accountable, and demand ethical behavior. By working together, both citizens and elected officials can rebuild trust and create a government that serves the interests of the people.

In conclusion, overcoming the deep state's influence requires a multifaceted approach that involves education, awareness, resistance, and active civic participation. By understanding their tactics, promoting transparency and accountability, and fostering unity, individuals can challenge the deep state's power and work towards a brighter future. It is a collective effort that requires the commitment and dedication of individuals who value freedom, democracy, and justice.

the deep state's motives and objectives of controlling the population and maintaining their power. This chapter has shed light on the dark and sinister agenda of the deep state, revealing their influence on politics, media, and the global economy. It has also explored the role of resistance and awareness in combating the deep state's control.

Now, in Section 11.4, we turn our attention to the crucial task of restoring trust in government. The deep state's actions have eroded the public's faith in the institutions that are meant to serve and protect them. The revelations of corruption, manipulation, and disregard for democratic values have left many feeling disillusioned and disconnected from their government.

Restoring trust in government requires a multifaceted approach that addresses the root causes of this erosion. It involves transparency, accountability, and a commitment to upholding the principles of democracy. Here, we will explore some key strategies for rebuilding trust and fostering a government that truly represents the interests of the people.

Transparency and Accountability

One of the fundamental pillars of restoring trust in government is transparency. The deep state's clandestine operations and hidden agendas have fueled suspicion and skepticism among the public. To counter this, government institutions must prioritize transparency in their actions and decision-making processes.

This means providing access to information, ensuring that government proceedings are open to public scrutiny, and actively engaging with citizens. Transparency also involves holding those in power accountable for their actions. This includes investigating and prosecuting instances of corruption, abuse of power, and other unethical behavior.

By promoting transparency and accountability, governments can demonstrate their commitment to serving the public interest and regain the trust that has been lost.

Citizen Engagement and Participation

Another crucial aspect of restoring trust in government is fostering citizen engagement and participation. When people feel disconnected from the decision-making processes that affect their lives, they are more likely to view the government with suspicion and mistrust.

Governments should actively seek input from citizens, listen to their concerns, and involve them in policy discussions. This can be achieved through town hall meetings, public consultations, and the use of technology to facilitate citizen engagement. By giving people a voice and actively involving them in the democratic process, governments can rebuild trust and demonstrate that they value the opinions and needs of their constituents.

Ethical Leadership and Integrity

Restoring trust in government also requires a commitment to ethical leadership and integrity. The deep state's actions have highlighted the dangers of unchecked power and corruption. To regain trust, government officials must lead by example and adhere to the highest ethical standards.

This involves promoting transparency in campaign financing, implementing strict conflict-of-interest regulations, and ensuring that public officials are held accountable for any unethical behavior. By demonstrating integrity and ethical conduct, leaders can rebuild trust and inspire confidence in the government's ability to serve the public interest.

Strengthening Democratic Institutions

To restore trust in government, it is essential to strengthen democratic institutions and safeguard the principles of democracy. This includes ensuring the independence of the judiciary, protecting freedom of the press, and promoting a vibrant civil society.

Governments should invest in the training and development of public servants, ensuring that they have the necessary skills and knowledge to effectively serve the public. Additionally, efforts should be made to promote diversity and inclusivity within government institutions, ensuring that they reflect the diverse voices and perspectives of the population.

By strengthening democratic institutions, governments can create a system that is resilient to the influence of the deep state and that upholds the values of democracy.

Rebuilding the Social Contract

Restoring trust in government ultimately requires rebuilding the social contract between the government and the people. This involves demonstrating that the government is working in the best interests of the citizens and that their rights and liberties are protected.

Governments must prioritize the well-being of their citizens, addressing their needs and concerns. This includes providing access to quality healthcare, education, and social services. By delivering on these basic needs, governments can rebuild the social contract and demonstrate their commitment to the welfare of the people.

Conclusion

Restoring trust in government is a complex and challenging task. It requires a commitment to transparency, accountability, citizen engagement, ethical leadership, and the strengthening of democratic institutions. By taking these steps, governments can begin to rebuild the trust that has been lost and work towards a brighter future for democracy and freedom.

In the final section of this book, we will conclude our exploration of the deep state's agenda and the battle for freedom and democracy. We will discuss the need for continued vigilance, empowering the people, and the call to action that is necessary to confront and overcome the deep state's influence. Together, we can strive for a future where transparency, accountability, and democratic values prevail.

Conclusion

the deep state's motives and objectives of controlling the population and maintaining their power. This chapter has shed light on the various tactics employed by the deep state, including their influence on politics, media manipulation, and economic control. It has also explored the global reach of the deep state and the importance of unmasking their actions.

As we conclude this book, it is crucial to emphasize the need for continued vigilance in the face of the deep state's agenda. The revelations presented throughout this book may be unsettling and challenging to accept, but it is essential to confront the truth in order to protect our freedoms and democracy.

The deep state operates in secrecy, using covert methods to achieve their objectives. They rely on the ignorance and complacency of the general population to maintain their control. Therefore, it is our responsibility as informed citizens to remain vigilant and stay informed about the actions and intentions of those in power.

Vigilance requires a commitment to seeking the truth and questioning the narratives presented to us. We must not blindly accept information from the mainstream media or government sources. Instead, we should engage in independent research, fact-checking, and critical thinking to uncover the hidden agendas and manipulations.

Furthermore, it is crucial to stay connected with like-minded individuals who share our concerns and beliefs. Building a community of individuals who are aware of the deep state's actions can provide support, encouragement, and a platform for sharing information. Together, we can amplify our voices and work towards exposing the truth.

In addition to vigilance, empowering the people is another essential aspect of countering the deep state's influence. This empowerment begins with education. We must educate ourselves and others about the tactics and strategies employed by the deep state. By understanding their methods, we can better recognize their actions and resist their control.

Empowerment also involves active participation in our democratic processes. We must exercise our rights as citizens by voting, engaging in peaceful protests, and holding our elected officials accountable. By actively participating in our democracy, we can ensure that our voices are heard and that the deep state's agenda is challenged.

However, it is important to note that resistance should be peaceful and within the boundaries of the law. The deep state thrives on chaos and division, and resorting to violence or illegal activities only plays into their hands. We must remain united, focused, and committed to non-violent means of resistance.

Lastly, this book concludes with a call to action. It is not enough to simply be aware of the deep state's agenda; we must actively work towards dismantling their power structures and restoring trust in our government. This can be achieved through grassroots movements, advocacy for transparency and accountability, and supporting political candidates who prioritize the interests of the people over the deep state's agenda.

Hope for a brighter future lies in our collective efforts to expose the deep state and reclaim our democracy. By remaining vigilant, empowering ourselves and others, and taking action, we can create a society that values truth, justice, and the preservation of our democratic values.

In conclusion, the deep state's agenda is real, and its impact on our society cannot be ignored. The need for continued vigilance is paramount in order to protect our freedoms, democracy, and the well-being of future generations. Let us stand together, united in our pursuit of truth, justice, and a brighter future for all.

the deep state's motives and objectives of controlling the population and maintaining their power. This book has shed light on the dark and hidden agenda of the deep state, revealing the truth behind their actions and the consequences they have on our society.

In this final section, "Empowering the People," we will explore the importance of knowledge, awareness, and action in the face of the deep state's influence. It is crucial for individuals to understand the power they possess and the role they can play in resisting and dismantling the deep state's agenda.

The Power of Knowledge

Knowledge is the foundation of empowerment. By understanding the deep state's tactics, motives, and objectives, individuals can arm themselves with the information needed to protect their rights and liberties. This book has provided a comprehensive analysis of the deep state's operations, revealing the truth behind their actions. It is now up to the readers to spread this knowledge and educate others about the hidden forces at play.

The Importance of Awareness

Awareness is the key to recognizing the signs of the deep state's influence. By staying informed and vigilant, individuals can identify the manipulation and propaganda techniques employed by the deep state and its media allies. This awareness allows people to question the narratives presented to them and seek alternative sources of information. It is through awareness that individuals can break free from the chains of media influence and think critically about the world around them.

Taking Action

Empowerment goes beyond knowledge and awareness; it requires action. It is not enough to simply be aware of the deep state's agenda; individuals must actively resist and work towards dismantling their power structures. This can be achieved through various means, such as peaceful protests, grassroots movements, and engaging in local politics. By coming together as a united front, individuals can amplify their voices and demand accountability from those in power.

Building a Resistance Movement

To effectively challenge the deep state's influence, it is essential to build a strong resistance movement. This movement should be inclusive, diverse, and united in its goal of restoring democracy and protecting individual rights. By organizing and mobilizing, individuals can create a collective force that cannot be ignored. This can involve forming alliances with like-minded organizations, supporting whistleblowers, and advocating for transparency and accountability in government.

Protecting Our Rights and Liberties

The deep state's agenda poses a significant threat to our rights and liberties. It is crucial for individuals to actively defend and protect these fundamental principles. This can be done through legal means, such as supporting organizations that fight for civil liberties, staying informed about legislation that impacts individual rights, and engaging in peaceful activism. By standing up for our rights, we send a clear message to the deep state that we will not allow them to erode our freedoms.

The Power of Unity

Unity is a powerful force that can bring about real change. By setting aside differences and focusing on common goals, individuals can create a united front against the deep state's influence. This unity can transcend political affiliations and ideologies, as the fight for freedom and democracy is a shared responsibility. By working together, we can overcome the deep state's grip on power and restore trust in our government.

Hope for a Brighter Future

Despite the dark and sinister nature of the deep state's agenda, there is always hope for a brighter future. The power lies within the people to challenge and dismantle the deep state's influence. By empowering ourselves with knowledge, awareness, and action, we can create a society that values transparency, accountability, and individual rights. It is through our collective efforts that we can pave the way for a better and more just world.

In conclusion, "Empowering the People" is a call to action. It is a reminder that we, as individuals, hold the power to challenge and dismantle the deep state's agenda. By arming ourselves with knowledge, staying aware, and taking action, we can build a resistance movement that protects our rights and liberties. Together, we can create a future where transparency, accountability, and democracy prevail. The fight against the deep state is not an easy one, but with determination and unity, we can overcome their influence and pave the way for a brighter future.

the deep state's motives and objectives of controlling the population and maintaining their power. This book has shed light on the dark and hidden agenda of the deep state, revealing the truth behind their actions and the consequences they have on our society.

In this final section, "A Call to Action," we must acknowledge the gravity of the situation we find ourselves in. The revelations presented in this book may be shocking and unsettling, but they are necessary for us to understand the depth of the problem we face. It is not enough to simply be aware of the deep state's agenda; we must take action to protect our rights, liberties, and the future of our democracy.

First and foremost, we must continue to educate ourselves and others about the deep state and its tactics. Knowledge is power, and by understanding the methods used to manipulate and control us, we can better resist their influence. Share this book with friends, family, and colleagues, encouraging them to read and discuss its contents. Engage in open and honest conversations about the deep state, its motives, and the impact it has on our lives.

Building a resistance movement is crucial in our fight against the deep state. We must come together as a united front, transcending political affiliations and personal differences. The deep state thrives on division and discord, so it is imperative that we find common ground and work towards a common goal – the preservation of our democracy and the protection of our individual freedoms.

One way to build a resistance movement is through grassroots organizing. Connect with like-minded individuals in your community and form local groups dedicated to raising awareness and taking action against the deep state. Host town hall meetings, organize peaceful protests, and engage in peaceful civil disobedience when necessary. By mobilizing at the local level, we can create a powerful force that cannot be ignored.

Another important aspect of our call to action is the protection of our rights and liberties. We must be vigilant in defending the principles upon which our nation was founded. Stay informed about proposed legislation and policies that could infringe upon our constitutional rights. Contact your elected representatives, attend public hearings, and make your voice heard. Together, we can hold our government accountable and ensure that our rights are protected.

In addition to protecting our rights, we must also work towards restoring trust in our government. The deep state's influence has eroded public confidence in our institutions, leading to widespread disillusionment and apathy. We must actively participate in the democratic process, holding our elected officials accountable and demanding transparency and integrity in government. Support candidates who prioritize the interests of the people over the interests of the deep state. By actively engaging in politics, we can begin to rebuild trust and create a government that truly represents the will of the people.

Lastly, we must not lose hope. While the revelations in this book may be disheartening, we must remember that we have the power to effect change. History has shown us that when people come together and stand up against injustice, they can overcome even the most formidable adversaries. We must remain steadfast in our commitment to truth, justice, and the preservation of our democratic values.

In conclusion, the deep state's agenda is real, and its impact on our society cannot be ignored. However, by taking action and working together, we can resist their influence and protect our rights and liberties. This book has provided us with the knowledge and understanding necessary to confront the deep state head-on. Now, it is up to us to heed the call to action and fight for a brighter future. Let us stand united, empowered, and unwavering in our pursuit of truth, justice, and a government that serves the people.

the deep state's motives and objectives of controlling the population and maintaining their power. This book has shed light on the dark and hidden agenda of the deep state, revealing the truth behind their actions and the consequences they have on our society.

However, amidst the revelations and the grim reality that has been exposed, there is still hope for a brighter future. It is essential to acknowledge that the fight against the deep state is not an easy one, but it is a fight that can be won. In this final section, we will explore the reasons for hope and the steps we can take to create a better tomorrow.

The Power of Unity

One of the most significant sources of hope lies in the power of unity. Throughout history, we have seen how collective action and solidarity have brought about significant change. When individuals come together, their voices become stronger, and their impact becomes greater. By uniting against the deep state's agenda, we can create a force that cannot be ignored.

It is crucial to build bridges and find common ground with individuals who may have different perspectives or beliefs. By focusing on shared values and goals, we can create a united front against the deep state's influence. This unity can extend beyond borders, as people from all around the world face similar challenges and aspirations. Together, we can work towards a future free from the grip of the deep state.

The Power of Education and Awareness

Another source of hope lies in the power of education and awareness. As more people become informed about the deep state's agenda and tactics, they can make informed decisions and take action to protect their rights and liberties. Education is a powerful tool that can empower individuals to question the status quo, think critically, and seek the truth.

By spreading awareness through various channels, such as social media, grassroots movements, and alternative media outlets, we can reach a broader audience and expose the deep state's actions. It is essential to encourage open dialogue and provide platforms for individuals to share their experiences and knowledge. Through education and awareness, we can dismantle the deep state's control over information and empower individuals to make informed choices.

The Power of Grassroots Movements

Grassroots movements have proven time and again to be catalysts for change. These movements, driven by passionate individuals who are committed to a cause, have the power to challenge the deep state's influence and bring about meaningful transformation. Grassroots movements can mobilize communities, raise awareness, and put pressure on those in power to address the concerns of the people.

By organizing peaceful protests, engaging in civil disobedience, and advocating for policy changes, grassroots movements can create a groundswell of support that cannot be ignored. These movements can also provide a platform for individuals to come together, share their stories, and find strength in their collective voice. Through grassroots movements, we can reclaim our power and demand accountability from those who seek to control us.

The Power of Technology

In today's digital age, technology has become a powerful tool for change. The internet and social media platforms have provided avenues for individuals to connect, share information, and organize. These platforms have the potential to amplify our voices and reach a global audience.

By utilizing technology responsibly and strategically, we can expose the deep state's actions, share alternative narratives, and mobilize support. It is crucial to remain vigilant against attempts to control or manipulate these platforms and to protect our digital rights and privacy. Technology can be a powerful ally in the fight against the deep state, but it must be used wisely and ethically.

The Power of Hope

Finally, hope itself is a powerful force that can drive us forward. It is easy to become overwhelmed by the revelations and challenges we face, but hope reminds us that change is possible. Hope fuels our determination, resilience, and belief in a better future.

By holding onto hope, we can inspire others to join the fight, create momentum for change, and overcome the obstacles that lie ahead. Hope reminds us that we are not alone in this battle and that together, we can build a brighter future for ourselves and future generations.

In conclusion, while the deep state's agenda may seem daunting and insurmountable, there is hope for a brighter future. Through unity, education, grassroots movements, technology, and the power of hope, we can challenge the deep state's influence and create a society that values freedom, justice, and democracy. The fight against the deep state is not an easy one, but it is a fight worth fighting. Let us stand together, empowered and determined, as we work towards a future where the shadows of power no longer cast a dark cloud over our lives.

www.ingramcontent.com/pod-product-compliance
Lightning Source LLC
Chambersburg PA
CBHW070855260726
48661CB00004B/1416